P9-DXM-661

D0037801

NEW ART IN AMERICA

NEW ART
in AMERICA

Fifty Painters of the 20th Century

BY John I. H. Baur, Editor

    Lloyd Goodrich

    Dorothy C. Miller

    James Thrall Soby

    Frederick S. Wight

PUBLISHED BY NEW YORK GRAPHIC SOCIETY
GREENWICH, CONN. IN COOPERATION
WITH FREDERICK A. PRAEGER, INC., NEW YORK

Photo-Offset Smeets Weert, the Netherlands

CONTENTS

FOREWORD

THIS BOOK is a joint adventure in which five authors, working closely together, have attempted to choose the fifty leading painters in 20th-century American art. None of us, I think, would have felt inclined to advance our individual selections as more than personal opinion. The fact that these names were finally chosen, after much soul-searching, by five people whose lives are all spent in the study of modern art is still no guarantee that mistakes have not been made, but at least it lessens the likelihood of prejudice. As a matter of fact, about two-thirds of our choices were unanimous—these being, for the most part, established artists, several of them now dead—and we are not so humble as to believe that time will soon reverse our estimate of them. The difficulty, as always, came with the younger painters and with certain others whose quality has a narrower appeal. We are all sure that if this group were to be selected again five years hence, it would include many different names. But we also believe that, while judgments are difficult in a field so near us in time, there is still no excuse for avoiding them.

These, then, are the fifty painters who did the most, we believe, to form American art in the 20th century. This is not quite the same as saying "the best," since there are a few men here who made fruitful innovations that affected the course of our painting but who did not, themselves, live up to their individual promise. In most cases, however, quality and importance are closely linked, and the enduring influences have been those that sprang from high creative ability.

Only after our selection was completed did we face the problem of who should write on whom. We had decided from the beginning to abandon any thought of a continuous text or even a consistent approach. Rather, the book was conceived as a series of essays which would draw without restriction on the large fund of knowledge and understanding represented by the five contributors. Artists were assigned, so far as possible, to those authors who had already made a special study of their work, but it would be a mistake to assume that the ten artists treated by each contributor represent his exclusive choice. The truth is that our preferences and enthusiasms overlapped at many points.

The book has been divided into three chronological sections with brief introductions by the editor. Artists have been grouped according to the period in which they did their first notable work, though usually both earlier and later paintings by each are illustrated. This is a fairly arbitrary order, but it has at least the advantage of bringing together men who reached artistic maturity in the same generation. From all living painters we have tried to get new statements of their aims, methods and convictions. A few—with the artist's congenital dislike of writing—have declined, but the majority have contributed generously to the book.

Many of the pioneers in our 20th-century painting are now dead. They have been succeeded through five-and-a-half decades by the most varied, numerous and intensely serious artists which this country has ever produced in so short a span. The battles of the advanced and conservative trends have been fought all through these years, and are still being fought today. More important, it seems to us, is the high level of individual achievement which our turbulent age has already produced. It is this, at its highest, that we have tried to present in the following pages.

John I. H. Baur

ACKNOWLEDGMENTS   So many people have helped in the realization of this book that it is impossible to thank them all personally. But I am especially grateful to the artists and their dealers who contributed so much time, thought and knowledge to the preparation of their respective sections. I am equally grateful to the private collectors, museums and other institutions for permitting their paintings to be reproduced here. In the case of the color reproductions, this involved the considerable inconvenience of allowing our photographer, Mr. Frank Lerner, to invade their premises, or of sending their pictures to a nearby museum to have the necessary separations made. The Art Institute of Chicago and the Whitney Museum of American Art were particularly kind in lending their facilities for color work on other than their own paintings, while the Museum of Modern Art unpacked an exhibition that was about to leave for Europe in order that a number of paintings owned by it and its trustees might be done in color.

The only set of color photographs not made specifically for this book were those of George Bellows' *Both Members of This Club,* lent through the generosity of the National Gallery of Art in Washington. One artist, Edwin Dickinson, preferred not to have his work reproduced in color, a wish which we have reluctantly respected.

I owe a personal debt of gratitude to all my fellow authors in this venture. Their suggestions and advice on the pattern of the whole book were as valuable as the texts and illustrations for which they were directly responsible. I would like to thank also Miss Marie Lenfest and Miss Penelope Platt of the Whitney Museum staff for all they did in the production of the book. Finally to my wife, Louise C. Baur, goes my gratitude for unfailing help and encouragement.

J. I. H. B.

NEW

DISCOVERIES

1900-1920

Sloan

Glackens

Bellows

Pickett

Eilshemius

Prendergast

Marin

Demuth

Feininger

Stella

Weber

Hartley

Dove

Macdonald-Wright

Ray

EARLY IN THE 20th century American artists made two profoundly important discoveries—one, that American life held rich material for the painter, which had not yet been explored; the other, that art could be built out of pure form and color alone. Nearly all American painting since then has been deeply affected by one or both of these twin forces, often by their conflict and interaction.

American life had, of course, been the subject of many American painters in preceding generations. From Mount and Bingham in the first half of the 19th century to Homer and Eakins, who worked well into the 20th, genre painting—the portrayal of scenes from everyday life—was a popular branch of art. But our traditional genre suffered from two serious disabilities. In the first place it had never, with a few exceptions, done more than scratch the surface of America's complex society. In the East it had dealt almost entirely with the smiling aspects of rural life; in the West with adventure and the frontier. In the second place, it had lost its creative vigor as time went on. Homer and Eakins abandoned it early in their careers. Their lesser contemporaries—men like J. G. Brown, Thomas Hovenden and E. L. Henry—pushed it in the direction of a nostalgic sentimentality. By 1900 genre painting was pretty thoroughly divorced from reality, and particularly from the urban reality of American life.

It was, therefore, essentially a new discovery when, early in the 20th century, a group of young painters turned for their subjects to the pattern of common existence in New York—to its movie houses, shops, parks and restaurants, its varied and strident humanity. Sloan, Glackens, Bellows and the other social realists, as they came to be called, painted the city not because it was new, but because they were genuinely in love with it. They painted it directly, with warmth and gusto, and in doing so they restored to genre its spontaneity and its essential truth. Believing with Robert Henri that art "is the trace of those who have led their lives," they worked from personal knowledge and experience; through their example they broadened and revitalized the nativist philosophy of art which had been common in the early 19th century and which was to flower again in the 1920's and '30's.

It was a different group of American painters that discovered in European modernism the then revolutionary concept of art as pure form (abstraction) and the only slightly less radical use of free distortions for emotional effect (expressionism). The formal values of art were not, of course, unknown in 19th-century America. From Allston to La Farge, the late Renaissance traditions of color and design had influenced many of our artists in various ways. Furthermore, it was generally conceded in our esthetic theory of the time that the painter had the right to alter nature for expressive effect and to distort visual reality in order to give it emotional meaning. But it is important to realize how strict were the limits imposed and accepted in a century dominated by naturalism. Men like Quidor, Ryder and Blakelock, who carried distortion beyond these limits, were doomed to neglect through most of their lives. To some extent this was true in European painting also, but there the pattern began to change during the century's last quarter. In France, the postimpressionists sought to transform the visual realism of impressionism into an art of stronger formal values, and in doing so they started an orderly evolution which led to cubism, fauvism and thence to the whole broad field of modern abstract and expressionist art.

In America no such logical development took place. There had always been a time lag between European innovations and their influence on American art. By the 1890's our painters were just beginning to experiment rather timidly with the pointillism of the French impressionists. Only a decade later a sizeable group of young American artists studying in Paris were converted, one after another, to the most extreme forms of modernism—that is, to cubism and fauvism—starting at almost the very moment that these new movements emerged in 1905–08. By 1913 a large selection of modern European painting had been brought to this country for the famous Armory Show, which extended the influence of abstract and expressionist art to a still wider circle. In those few years at the opening of the century we wiped out the traditional delay of nearly a generation between European and American art forms, but in doing so we skipped the whole quarter-century of experiment which had led to the birth of modernism abroad. The result was a revolution rather than an evolution for both the American artist and the American public.

It is apparent that our twin discoveries of the early 1900's—the artistic resources of American life and the formal language of art—tended to pull artists in opposite directions. To the social realists, design was principally a means for telling a story or creating mood. Stylistically the social realists were not venturesome, being content, for the most part, with the broad, painterly handling which they had inherited from Duveneck, Chase and Henri. The quality that gave their work enduring vitality was their enthusiasm for the new vein in American life which they were exploring—an enthusiasm tinged with humor, satire and an immense relish for the unconventional aspects of humanity that the city afforded. Their art was colloquial and dramatic, but it was seldom distinguished in a formal sense.

One could scarcely find a greater contrast than the work of those American modernists who discarded all subject matter for abstract design, or who wrenched it into the distortions of expressionism. Their anonymous figures, still lifes, compositions and collages laid no claim to a distinctively American quality although, as we shall see, they had their own character which was often quite different from European work in the same vein. But the point is that these young Americans felt they were breaking away from native tradition, not trying to revitalize it, that they were embarking on an international experiment and creating a new art form that had no connection with their past. To all appearances, their motivations and directions were diametrically opposed to those of the social realists.

Yet as time goes by and we see the early years of the century in better perspective, the oppositions begin to seem less important and certain underlying bonds emerge more clearly. For one thing, most of the American modernists were not willing to go so far as Macdonald-Wright, for instance, in giving up subject matter entirely. It was too long a first step and led, perhaps, into too frightening a void. Many, like Feininger and Weber, stayed generally within semi-abstract limits, keeping recognizable elements of nature in their strongly patterned canvases—as indeed the cubists themselves had done at the beginning. Others, like Dove and Hartley, built their abstractions about symbols which suggested meanings and moods beyond purely esthetic ones. Furthermore, many of the modernists returned to America and became as deeply concerned with its character and its spirit as the social realists. Often the interests of the two groups converged closely. The city had the same fascination for Marin,

Stella and Weber that it had for Sloan, Glackens and Bellows. There was, of course, a difference: the social realists were chiefly concerned with its human drama, the modernists with its soaring buildings, its lights, its tempo, its total impact on the senses. But in a very real sense, these were only opposite sides of the same coin. Both groups were spiritually akin in their romantic response to the city's aliveness and in their common attempt to express its dynamic vitality.

Dynamism, while a dangerously vague word, offers, indeed, the best single description of the predominant quality in the creative art of this country during the early years of the century. It applies not only to the drama of the city as it was interpreted by both modernists and realists, but also to a large part of our early abstract painting which dealt with entirely different themes. It is significant that the two European movements which had the greatest influence on American artists at this time were Orphism and futurism, and both of these were attempts to infuse dynamic motion into the relatively static patterns of cubism. The American Synchromist movement, founded by Morgan Russell and Macdonald-Wright, was so similar in its aims and methods to Orphism that there was no practical difference between them. Both used color relations to create a sense of depth and of receding or advancing planes. Futurism was even more deeply concerned with motion, which it depicted by graphic symbols such as curving force lines or repeated chevrons. It had a close follower here in Joseph Stella and exerted an appreciable influence on Demuth, Feininger, Weber and a number of lesser men. Even the comparatively flat abstractions of Hartley and Dove, which seem at first glance closer to cubism, are full of strong tensions which thrust against the plane of the picture and create conflicting movements. In other words the Americans turned instinctively to the more dynamic and romantic forms of European abstraction, and while they followed these closely at times, more often they devised their own modifications which further heightened the dynamism.

Today the individual experiments of the American modernists seem to have much in common, but historically they never coalesced (except for Synchromism's brief life) into a well-defined movement with an articulate program, an acknowledged leader, a clear-cut membership or an official apologist. That was the European pattern, not the American. Alfred Stieglitz gave them faithful support at his small 291 Gallery, and a few others helped from time to time. But for the most part the Americans had to fight a piecemeal battle against public indifference, general misunderstanding and violent professional hostility. Even the social realists had been greeted as "apostles of ugliness" in a country still dominated by an academic art of polite conventions; the abstract and expressionist painters were "madmen" or "charlatans." It is small wonder that many of them became discouraged and that a widespread reaction set in soon after the close of the first World War. In a different cultural climate the results might have been otherwise, for the solid accomplishment of our pioneer modernists looks more impressive today than it did in their own time or in the period of reaction following it. Indeed it begins to appear that they created an art which was considerably more than the sum of their borrowings, and peculiarly related to the American mind of that generation.

SLOAN: *Hairdresser's Window,* 1907.

Oil, 32 x 26. Wadsworth Atheneum, Hartford.

JOHN SLOAN 13

JOHN SLOAN *by Lloyd Goodrich*

THE ACADEMIC idealism of the American art world at the turn of the century was broken by a group of young realists, Robert Henri, George Luks, William Glackens, John Sloan and Everett Shinn, all Philadelphians, all close friends, all students of the Pennsylvania Academy, and all except Henri originally newspaper artists. Their leader was the oldest, Henri—brilliant, magnetic and a born teacher. He encouraged them to paint, he confirmed their bent toward the life around them, he opened their eyes to the great realists of the past, Velasquez, Hals, Rembrandt, Goya, Daumier and Manet.

Rebelling against academic sweetness and light, the Henri group turned to the life of the modern city (at first Philadelphia, later New York, where all of them settled). They loved the city as their nineteenth-century predecessors had loved the country. Their relish for low life, their satirical humor and their social conscience were new notes in American painting. And not only in their art did they combat academicism: for two decades they spearheaded the battle for artistic independence and against academic domination of the art world. In alliance with other progressive and modern artists, they were leaders in such events as the Armory Show.

John Sloan, next to youngest of the group and, with Glackens, the most gifted, was born in 1871 at Lock Haven, Pennsylvania, brought up in Philadelphia, and became a successful newspaper artist. Under Henri's influence he began to paint seriously when he was twenty-six; but his career as painter and etcher really started when he moved to New York in 1904, fell in love with the city, and became its leading realistic interpreter of the time.

Sloan's chief motivating force was his interest in human beings. He liked what was common, everyday and universal; he liked the places and occasions when people got together; he liked character, the humors of daily life, and the infinite variety of a great city. He preferred the masses to the upper classes. His art had

SLOAN: *Three A.M.*, 1909.

Oil, 32 x 26. Philadelphia Museum of Art.

that quality of being a direct product of ordinary reality, authentic and full of flavor, that has marked the best genre art of all periods. He had a singularly true eye, and his style from the first was delightful in its fresh

JOHN SLOAN   15

16

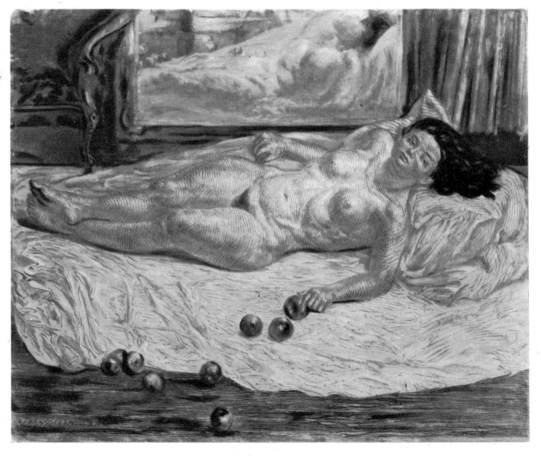

SLOAN:

Sixth Avenue Elevated at Third Street, 1928.

Oil, 30 x 40. Whitney Museum of American Art.

observation and racy graphic sense. Though his satire of wealth and pretence could be sharp, on the whole his was a kindly humor, without the bitterness of the following generation of social realists. His art was fundamentally affirmative, based on a deep and warm love of humanity—not in the abstract but in the individual. And he loved the city for itself, its moods in different seasons, weathers and times of day. With all his realism, he was a poet who found his beauty all around him, in the everyday life of city streets.

When Sloan was nearing sixty, an age when most artists are through with experimenting, he completely transformed his art—in subjects, style and technique. Abandoning the contemporary scene, he concentrated on the figure, and especially the female nude. His chief aim became the realization of sculptural form, using the technique of the old masters. These figure pieces of his last twenty years, though without the humor and human interest of his early work, were among the strongest plastic creations of our time in America; they have a sort of tough idiosyncrasy, and the solid existence that all lasting art has.

In his long, hard-working, often embattled life Sloan combined several careers: illustrator, painter, etcher, pioneer socialist, art editor of *The Masses,* chief organizer of early independent shows, perennial president of the Society of Independent Artists, and one of the greatest teachers of his generation. For many years before his death in 1951 he was a leading citizen of the American art world.

Sloan: *Nature is what you see plus what you think about it. . . . The artist's mental image of the thing seen in nature, expressed in graphic terms, is what gives creative vitality to the work.* (John Sloan, *Gist of Art,* 1939, p. 40)

See: John Sloan (with Helen Farr), *Gist of Art,* 1939. Lloyd Goodrich, *John Sloan,* 1952. Van Wyck Brooks, *John Sloan,* 1955.

JOHN SLOAN 17

WILLIAM J. GLACKENS

by Lloyd Goodrich

BORN IN PHILADELPHIA in 1870, Glackens like his friends Sloan, Luks and Shinn began as a newspaper artist, painting in his spare time under Henri's inspiring influence. After a year abroad in 1895 he settled in New York and became a successful free-lance illustrator. He was a born draftsman (Sloan said "he could draw anything"), commanding a line that was keen, delicate and alive, and his illustrations rank among the best American graphic art.

His early paintings, as with the others of the Henri group, were reportorial: their subject-matter was New York. But whereas Sloan and Luks preferred the common life, Glackens inclined toward the upper levels of society. He liked elegant women, stylish promenaders on Fifth Avenue, Central Park with its carriages and children and nursemaids, night life in restaurants and roof gardens, and the whole spectacle of city life; and he painted all this with gaiety, style, a love of movement and color, and an incisive sense of character. Where Sloan had humor, Glackens had wit. Everything in his work was alive: basically graphic, it gave just the essentials; it proved that in paint as in words, brevity is the soul of wit. Charm is a much-abused word, but Glackens' early work possessed it, genuinely.

In their youth all the Henri group were in conscious revolt against impressionism—or rather what impressionism had become in America, pretty and academic. The style of their early work—bold, graphic, dark in palette, with prevailing grays, browns and blacks—was a return to what they felt was the truer realistic tradition of Velasquez, Hals, Goya, and the pre-impressionist Manet. Like the others, Glackens in early years deliberately restricted his palette to cool silvery grays and rich blacks, with only an occasional stronger note.

A turning-point in Glackens' career came with a visit to France and Spain in 1906, when his painting showed the obvious impact of Manet and Renoir. In the next few years his work went through basic changes. His subjects broadened out into landscape, figure-painting, the nude, still-life—the full range of the painter's immemorial themes. His art became an expression of pagan love of sunlight, summer, the human body, children, flowers. Everything was bathed in all-embracing light. Abandoning the grays of early years, his color blossomed into the full impressionist gamut, used with an opulence rare in American art. His pictures, like those of his greatest admiration, Renoir, seemed drenched in color. But his style never entirely lost its graphic character—its observation, vivacity and sense of movement. By contrast with the academic American followers of impressionism, who exploited its naturalistic side, Glackens belonged in its more creative current, which led to postimpressionism and the modern movements.

After his early years Glackens was blessed with an assured income and could devote himself to his great love, painting. He went abroad many times and worked much in France, especially in the South. In the fight for artistic independence he played a quiet but effective part, as chairman for selection of American works for the Armory Show, and as the first president of the Society of Independent Artists. Before his death in 1938 he had received many awards and honors.

Glackens: *"Artists say the silliest things about painting."* (Quoted in Guy Pène du Bois, *Artists Say the Silliest Things,* 1940, p. 192.)

See: Forbes Watson, William Glackens, *The Arts,* Apr. 1923, pp. 246–261. Whitney Museum of American Art, *William Glackens Memorial Exhibition,* 1938.

GLACKENS: *The Soda Fountain,* 1935.

Oil, 48 x 36. Pennsylvania Academy of the Fine Arts.

GLACKENS: *Chez Mouquin*, 1905.

Oil, 48 x 39. Art Institute of Chicago.

GLACKENS:

Hammerstein's Roof Garden, c. 1901.

    Oil, 30 x 25. Whitney Museum of American Art.

GLACKENS:

Central Park, Winter, c. 1905.

    Oil, 25 x 30. Metropolitan Museum of Art.

21

GEORGE BELLOWS

by Frederick S. Wight

BELLOWS was the most important figure in a group that came to be called the Ash Can School. These men, like the Fauves in France, opened the century gustily, enjoying the satisfaction of revolt. But the American revolution was in subject matter. Its painters were realists, most of whom had worked as illustrators on the daily press. Their assault was against the proprieties, in the name of humanity and truth.

Bellows was as American as Theodore Roosevelt. He could convey action, he could throw limelight into his paintings. He could arrest attention. He was an athlete. Born in Columbus, Ohio, in 1882, he had a college career in baseball at Ohio State, and he took a natural interest in the prize ring long before burliness became a cult.

He came to New York to paint, studied under Robert Henri, and bettered his teacher's direct vision and attack. His genial instinct for leadership and success carried him to the fore, and he was soon abreast of his

BELLOWS: *River Front, No. 1,* 1915.

Oil, 45 x 63. Columbus Gallery of Fine Arts.

BELLOWS: *Elinor, Jean and Anna*, 1920.

Oil, 59 x 66. Albright Art Gallery.

elders. The first painting he sold was his *Forty-two Kids* of 1907. His *Stag at Sharkey's* of the next year shows him at the height of his early innocent style when his painting had the characteristics of a sport. He was just twenty-three.

The times were to change radically. With the coming of the Armory Show in 1913 it was obvious that there was a new vanguard; heightened impact was no longer enough, and the battle was for ideas. Nothing daunted, Bellows reached for the new weapons and went in self-consciously for structure.

Unfortunately, he equipped himself with Hambidge's Dynamic Symmetry and the play of muscles was succeeded by the clank· of armor. With Dynamic Symmetry, Bellows tended to lose himself in triangulation, his figures stiffened in semaphore gestures, his dynamism departed and his canvases became set pieces. But there were times when he animated the dead weight of theory through sheer strength, and his paintings turned into monuments of controlled power. The *Dempsey and Firpo* fight substitutes stylized tension for the mobility of the *Stag at Sharkey's,* and like the press camera, cuts an instant of glare out of time.

Bellows was perhaps at his best painting the women of his family—more tender, less declamatory—his

floodlighting throwing a marvelous cohesion over the figures, and dramatizing the reality of flesh. He has to his credit the re-discovery of lithography, the perfect vehicle for his instinct for massed blacks and whites.

Bellows was always willing to vary his attack, to profit by spontaneity or to be thoughtful and painstaking. There was urgency, power, resource in his work and his essential youthfulness promised achievements ahead. He died suddenly in 1924. Already in 1930 Henry McBride was writing retrospectively. "Bellows had a simple and direct mind, not overly subtle, but the very directness of his thought made it impressive to his friends."

Bellows: *I have no desire to destroy the past. I am deeply moved by the great works of former times, but I refuse to be limited by them.*

There are no successful pictures without a geometrical basis. (From The Art Institute of Chicago, *George Bellows Paintings, ` Drawings, and Prints* exhibition catalogue, 1946, p. 23.)

See: George Bellows, *The Paintings of George Bellows,* 1929. George W. Eggers, *George Bellows,* 1931. Peyton Boswell, Jr., *George Bellows,* 1942.

BELLOWS: *Both Members of This Club*, 1909.

Oil, 45¼ x 63⅛. National Gallery of Art, Washington. Chester Dale Collection (Gift).

26

JOSEPH PICKETT

by Dorothy C. Miller

SOME YEARS after his death a village storekeeper named Joseph Pickett won sudden acclaim as an artist when Holger Cahill included two of his paintings, those later acquired by the Newark and Whitney Museums, in the exhibition *American Primitives* at the Newark Museum in 1930. Two years later Pickett's masterpiece, *Manchester Valley,* was purchased by Mrs. John D. Rockefeller, Jr. and shown with her collection of American folk art at the Museum of Modern Art in New York. Along with Edward Hicks, whose work was introduced in the same exhibitions, Pickett was drawn for the first time into the mainstream of American art.

Pickett had died in 1918 in New Hope, Pennsylvania, where he was born in 1848 and lived his life through. Old residents of the village, questioned by

PICKETT: *Manchester Valley,* probably 1914–18.

Oil, 45 x 60. Museum of Modern Art, gift of Mrs. John D. Rockefeller, Jr.

Holger Cahill and later by William Chapman, supplied the little that is known of Pickett, his personality and his work as a painter. No remark he may have made about his painting is remembered, nor is any letter or photograph of Pickett known to exist.

Pickett's father had a boatyard in New Hope, which is on the Delaware River and the Lehigh Canal. He and his sons were canal-boat builders but Joseph left the boatyard early. He was of a restless, lively and inventive turn of mind, a man who could build a house or a sailboat, make a chair or a pair of shoes, devise new kinds of tools, whittle toys, and finally paint a picture. His contemporaries described him as always getting into something new and handy at anything he tried. He kept a general store where he had a pool table and a shooting gallery. In the summers he used to travel about to country fairs and picnic grounds with his shooting gallery, for which he carved the targets and painted landscape backgrounds.

Pickett turned to serious painting late in life, probably at about sixty-five. He painted in the back room of the grocery store he kept at that time. He worked for a very long time on each picture, completing three large canvases which illustrate incidents in the history of his native town. He also painted a tree on the outside wall of his store, part of which was visible until the late 1930s when the building was renovated.

Pickett is said to have exhibited his paintings in his store window, but his only attempt to enter a formal exhibition was in 1918 when William Lathrop, a resident of the artist colony at New Hope, persuaded him to submit a picture to the jury at the Pennsylvania Academy's annual show in Philadelphia. The painting, probably *Manchester Valley,* was rejected but is said to have received the votes of Lathrop, Robert Henri and Robert Spencer.

After Pickett's death his belongings were sold at auction, but the paintings brought only a dollar each and his widow bought them in. She gave *Manchester Valley* to the New Hope schoolhouse, the building with a flag which appears in the painting. In 1925 the painter Lloyd Ney, returning from Paris, saw *Washington under the Council Tree* and *Coryell's Ferry* hanging in Worthington Brothers garage in New Hope and bought them for fifteen dollars. Later he traded the paintings to R. Moore Price of New Hope for frames. Shortly before the Newark Museum exhibition, Pickett's work is said to have had its first public showing at the New Hope Town Hall in an avant-garde show called "The New Group" organized about 1930 by C. F. Ramsey and Adolphe Blondheim.

PICKETT:

George Washington under the Council Tree, probably 1914–18.

Oil, 35 x 37½. Newark Museum.

It is surprising that a skilled artisan like Pickett, a man of inquiring mind always ready to experiment, did not start painting earlier in life. To the fortunate fact that he finally did paint we owe three of the most remarkable landscapes ever produced in America. Pickett had a freely arbitrary way of handling space and perspective and did not hesitate to invent his own methods of applying paint to suit the needs of the picture as he felt them. He had the clear and intense vision, unerring control of his medium, firm structure and sober harmony of color that characterize the work of the rare few among naive painters.

See: Museum of Modern Art, *American Folk Art,* exhibition catalogue by Holger Cahill, 1932, pp. 16, 33–34. Museum of Modern Art, *Masters of Popular Painting,* exhibition catalogue by Holger Cahill, Maximilien Gauthier and others, 1938, pp. 99–101, 123–124. Sidney Janis, *They Taught Themselves,* 1942, pp. 110–116.

PICKETT: *Coryell's Ferry, 1776*, probably 1914–18.
Oil, 37½ x 48. Whitney Museum of American Art.

LOUIS M. EILSHEMIUS

by Lloyd Goodrich

SELF-STYLED "Mahatma, Mightiest Mind and Wonder of the Worlds, Supreme Parnassian and Grand Transcendent Eagle of Art," Louis Michel Eilshemius in old age was an eccentric, embittered by a lifetime of neglect. But he did not begin this way. A "primitive," he was so only in the sense that his art was a spontaneous outlet for an original imagination, with scant regard to prevailing standards of taste or technique. Certainly he was no folk-painter: he was born of well-to-do parents (in 1864 in North Arlington, N. J.), went to college, studied art in New York and at the Académie Julian in Paris, travelled at various times in Europe, North Africa and the South Pacific, and was financially independent.

All his life Eilshemius remained an adolescent, with both the gifts and the limitations of adolescence—sensibility, naiveté, romantic fantasy. His early work was essentially impressionist, but not the academic brand that won prizes: his was a highly personal impressionism, responding to nature with the candor and freshness of youth. His landscapes were spontaneous, unconventional records of nature's moods, having at the same time an odd dreamlike quality, as if they pictured not the everyday scene but an inner world which was yet quite real to their creator. Often he peopled them with naked women, bathing, playing, disporting themselves—pure embodiments of the amorous dreams that haunt the adolescent mind. These innocent fantasies were barely saved from absurdity by their instinctive artistry. They had none of the true primitive's hard woodenness. The subtle pervading light, the tender springlike delicacy of the high-pitched colors, relieved by dark accents, the sensitive patterns, were products of an intuitive talent that, consciously or unconsciously,

EILSHEMIUS: *Bridge for Fishing,* c. 1905.

Oil, 18 x 35. Phillips Collection, Washington.

EILSHEMIUS:

Jealousy, 1915.

Oil, 19½ x 25. Henry Clifford.

LOUIS M. EILSHEMIUS   33

EILSHEMIUS: *Afternoon Wind*, 1899.
Oil, 20 x 36. Museum of Modern Art.

EILSHEMIUS: *Tragedy or Found Drowned,* 1916. Oil, 39½ x 60½. Miss Adelaide Milton de Groot.

found the inevitable forms to convey its vision. Even his awkwardness contributed to the sense of a youthful world where all emotions were fresh, all desires possible.

But these were not the qualities that pass academic juries, and after being accepted a few times in early days, Eilshemius' pictures were consistently rejected. For about thirty years he continued to paint without recognition of any kind. Partly due to this frustration, partly through the natural development of his romantic imagination, his art moved further away from the norm toward unbridled fantasy and a growing sense of tragedy. His gentle idyllicism was interrupted more and more by pictures of horror and tortured emotions, uninhibited in their violence. His drawing took on a frenzied freedom, his distortions grew wildly expressive. Drained of light, heavy with despair, his color became sombre, hot, arbitrary. His new dramatic quality often turned into melodrama, but its lurid banality was transcended by the force of a genuine inner anguish. This passionate inwardness places Eilshemius in the small company of authentic visionaries.

With the arrival of modernism Eilshemius finally received his due. In 1917 the juryless Independents gave him his first chance to exhibit in years. Hailed by advanced artists such as Marcel Duchamp, he was eventually taken up by dealers and treated seriously by critics. But the recognition came too late: in 1921 he had laid down his brushes for good. For twenty more years, until his death in 1941, he lived on, a querulous, pathetically self-glorifying old man—a clear case of overcompensation for the long years of neglect.

Eilshemius: *The artist does not learn from a set of books or a university course whether or not his painting is right. He can't discuss it or prove it, but when his impulse is stilled and his painting is finished he requires no instructor, no critic, no public, to certify that the result of his efforts is Art; for Art, like virtue, is its own reward, and the experience is divine.* (William Schack, *And He Sat among the Ashes,* 1939, p. 222.)

See: William Schack, *And He Sat among the Ashes,* 1939.

MAURICE PRENDERGAST

by Lloyd Goodrich

WHILE THE New York realists were continuing the naturalistic tradition of the nineteenth century, in Europe the modern movement was evolving a new concept of the nature of art: not as representation of reality, but as creation in the language of form, color and design—a visual language as directly sensuous as music. Of this revolution the first American pioneer, and for years the only one, was Maurice Prendergast.

Of mingled Irish and French ancestry, born either in Newfoundland in 1859 or in Boston in 1861 (no one knows which), Prendergast was brought up in the latter city. He and his younger brother Charles, the woodcarver and decorative artist, were devoted, and spent most of their lives together. With no regular art training, Maurice as a boy began to sketch outdoors. About 1892 he went to France for three or four years; and it must have been then that he got to know the art of Cézanne, whose first American admirer and champion he became. For years he had little recognition. Included in the famous 1908 show of The Eight, his work was the most violently attacked: one reviewer called it "an explosion in a color factory." His first success did not come until the Armory Show. His last ten years were spent in New York, where he died in 1924.

In early years Prendergast worked mostly in watercolor; all his subjects were outdoors, and he could not afford oil paints and canvas. His favorite motifs were the parks and playgrounds and bathing beaches in and around Boston, with gaily dressed women and children—pictures full of sunlight, air and breeze, the color and movement of crowds, flags flying, dappled light and shade—a holiday spirit as fresh and simple as a child's. These watercolors were a direct expression of the pure, uncomplicated pleasure of the eye. Instinctively Prendergast saw the world as patterns of shapes and hues pleasurable in themselves. He had a delicious color sense, a gift that cannot be learned but must be inborn,

PRENDERGAST: *South Boston*, 1896.

Watercolor, 18½ x 13½. Smith College Museum of Art.

MAURICE PRENDERGAST　　　　37

PRENDERGAST: *Autumn Festival*, 1917–18.
Oil, 24 x 28. Phillips Collection, Washington.

PRENDERGAST: *Central Park,* 1901.

Watercolor, 14⅛ x 21¾ . Whitney Museum of American Art.

like a musician's ear. In his naive way he was doing
what certain innovators abroad such as Bonnard and
Vuillard were doing—taking the impressionist discoveries of light and color, and creating with them an art
of free form and mood.

From the early 1900's Prendergast worked more in
oil, on a larger scale and in more complex compositions.
His subjects remained the same, but were now less
specific: women and children in parks, among trees,
with glimpses of distant water and ships sailing—an
idyllic world pervaded by the lyricism of youth, of
springtime and summer, yet with a twilight mood, as
evocative and haunting as the music of Debussy.

His style grew constantly freer from naturalistic limitations. The picture was now conceived as an overall
design in harmonic color and rhythmic line. The paint
was applied in varicolored touches, producing an inter-

weaving of hues like the woven threads of textiles—a
highly personal development of impressionist technique.
Prendergast loved pigment in itself, and in his hands
it became sensuously enjoyable. Through the years his
innate color sense grew both richer and subtler, and
his later paintings had the muted splendor of faded
tapestries.

Though he was never a powerful designer in round
form and deep space, Prendergast's art was purely
plastic. There was a fundamental difference between
him and most of his American contemporaries: with
them the physical elements of painting were means to
achieve representation, with him they were integral
parts of plastic design. He was the first American artist
of his time to see the picture as a physical object having
its own order and harmony—a concept which has governed modern art for the past half-century.

Prendergast: *"The love you liberate in your work is the only love you keep."* (Quoted by Van Wyck Brooks in the Addison Gallery catalogue, below.)

See: William Mathewson Milliken, Maurice Prendergast, American Artist, *The Arts,* Apr. 1926, pp. 180–192. The Addison Gallery of American Art, *The Prendergasts* exhibition catalogue, 1938. Charles Sawyer, The Prendergasts, *Parnassus,* Oct. 1938, pp. 9–11.

PRENDERGAST:

Bridge and Steps, Venice, 1912.

Watercolor, 19½ x 15. Norton Gallery and School of Art, West Palm Beach.

JOHN MARIN

by Frederick S. Wight

MARIN: *Woolworth Building, No. 31,* 1912.

Watercolor, 19½ x 16. Mrs. Eugene Meyer.

JOHN MARIN went to Europe and returned before he discovered America. This happened to him in middle life after long years of tentative essays. New and bolder means were needed to convey the raw, vivid country which he now saw. New York and Maine—steel and rock—with a feeling for motion sluicing through them or breaking over them—these were his subjects, and for the rest of his life he simplified his means of expression.

Marin was born in Rutherford, New Jersey, in 1870. His mother died at his birth, and he was brought up by two maiden aunts at Weehawken. School past, he worked in a wholesale notion house and then in an architect's office. He was twenty-eight when he took up art, passing for a failure at all else. He went to the Pennsylvania Academy for two years, wasted time over the motionless plaster cast, and was no further along five years out of art school. His father, relenting, sent him to Paris, but Marin somehow missed the excitement of the scene. A restless vagabondage, a few etchings in the vein of Whistler, a good game of billiards and watercolors intriguingly simplified were the net result. Steichen saw the paintings and took them home to Alfred Stieglitz, America's great impresario of modern art. Stieglitz showed the watercolors in New York, promoted Marin for many years, building a legend—a counter-legend to himself—out of Marin's aloof genius. It was through Stieglitz that Marin discovered the quintessence of European painting that he had missed abroad.

During the 1910's Marin worked out a new brittle shorthand in his watercolors. As in golf, he said, the fewest number of strokes won the game. These strokes he applied to New York City—the Woolworth Building, the Brooklyn Bridge—which had also been a target for his etching. In summer, he extended his frontier into New England, and finally discovered Maine. For many

MARIN: *Maine Islands,* 1922.

Watercolor, 16¾ x 20. Phillips Collection, Washington.

JOHN MARIN 43

MARIN: *Lower Manhattan,* 1920.

Watercolor, 21⅞ x 26⅞. Phillip L. Goodwin.

years Maine gave Marin what it gave Hartley, the elementals of sky, sea, rock and tree so clean and stark that he had his building materials in basic terms.

Marin aimed at the essential characteristic. "Pertaining to" in his titles—*Pertaining to Deer Isle*—describes his selective vision. Physically, Maine allowed him to become the pioneer in living that he had become in his work. As time went on Marin moved further and further East. He lived at Small Point beyond Portland from 1915 to 1920; went on to Stonington on the Atlantic side of Deer Isle until 1933, when he made a final remove to Cape Split, close to the rocky edge of the country. In winters he lived in Cliffside, on the Jersey Palisades, within sight of New York and not too far from his childhood home. He died in 1953.

In Marin, jigsaw patterns hint at a cubist origin, but actually the forms are dictated by the need of motion. Representation goes over into symbols for economy and speed. Marin was irked by the static monotony of the rectangular frame, and a few bold strokes, banking on the frame like billiard shots, enclosed the painting with an appropriate geometry. Composition, for him, works out as a controlled progression through a painting, a navigation from headland to headland.

For Marin, watercolor had provided the light baggage of the explorer. But he had always painted in oils, and by the 1940's the emphasis definitely shifted to the heavier medium, which better suited his needs. He now used oil paint for additional impact and power rather than for mass, and to a large degree he retained the

JOHN MARIN 45

OPPOSITE:

MARIN: *Two-master Becalmed, Maine,* 1923.

Watercolor, 16½ x 19½. Alfred Stieglitz Collection, Metropolitan Museum of Art.

MARIN: *Fir Tree, Deer Isle, Maine,* 1926.

Watercolor, 21¼ x 17¼. Newark Museum.

qualities of watercolor. In straining a medium to suit a purpose he became a pioneer again. The shift compared to his removal to Cape Split, to a bolder, lonelier region in place of the now-familiar, in quest of freedom, and a final frontier.

Marin: *I see rocks upriver and the water flowing. All right, I put down the rocks on my paper. Then I show how the water runs past the rocks. The water is more white than colored, you notice, but you have to use color—never mind what color—or you couldn't show how the water runs along on white paper. Now, I say to myself, the most important thing about a river is that it runs downhill. So I put on the color with strokes that show how the water runs downhill past the rocks. Simple, isn't it?*

The sea that I paint may not be the *sea, but it is a sea, not an abstraction.* (From MacKinley Helm, *John Marin Retrospective Exhibition* catalogue, Institute of Modern Art, Boston, 1947.)

See: E. M. Benson, *John Marin, the Man and his Work,* 1935. Museum of Modern Art, *John Marin, Water Colors, Oil Paintings, Etchings* exhibition catalogue, 1936. Institute of Contemporary Art, Boston, *John Marin, a Retrospective Exhibition* catalogue, 1947. MacKinley Helm, *John Marin,* 1949.

OPPOSITE:

MARIN: *Composition, Cape Split, Maine,* 1933.

Oil, 22 x 28. Mr. and Mrs. Lawrence A. Fleischman.

MARIN: *Tunk Mountains, Autumn, Maine*, 1945.
Oil, 25 x 30. Phillips Collection, Washington.

CHARLES DEMUTH

by James Thrall Soby

OF AMERICAN PAINTERS affected by the cubists' revolt, the most elegant and perhaps the most gifted was Charles Demuth (1883–1935), born in Lancaster, Pa., to an old and affluent family in whose house he spent much of his life, often tormented by illness but also needing, for psychological reasons, his birthplace's atmosphere of permanence and sanctuary. But he was not a recluse. On the contrary, his friends knew him as esthete, dandy and gourmet, fond of travel and public places, especially nightclubs and the theatre. Nevertheless, his art is essentially private, even secret; it stems from an aristocratic withdrawal of spirit which left him free to comment sharply, and with remarkable originality and skill, on subjects from life and literature that interested him deeply. He was most at ease with watercolor, a medium whose requirements of delicacy and precision suited his slender, firm hands.

Two trips to Paris before World War I gave him the basic ingredients of his style—cubism as to form, and the impact of such divergent masters as El Greco, Watteau, Fragonard, Blake, the Japanese printmakers, Lautrec and Beardsley in questions of designs. In his figure pieces (which are quite likely his greatest works), he often used Mannerist distortions of contour and tensions of pose. His still lifes of flowers, vegetables and fruit, on the other hand, are sometimes presented as though seen imbedded in the most flawless ice, glistening and hypnotically quiet. And when he painted architectural scenes, he was not ashamed to include romantic-atmospheric effects, laced taut by cubism's grammar and his own impeccable taste. He was fond of paradox and irony, and therefore inevitably became a friend of Marcel Duchamp during the war years in New York. Though never a Dadaist in an official sense,

DEMUTH: *Acrobats,* 1919.

Watercolor, 13 x 7⅜. Museum of Modern Art, gift of Mrs. John D. Rockefeller, Jr.

DEMUTH: *In Vaudeville,* 1918.

Watercolor, 11 x 8. Mr. and Mrs. Samuel S. White, III.

DEMUTH:

Purple Pup, I, c. 1918.

Watercolor, 8 x 11. Downtown Gallery.

DEMUTH: *End of the Parade: Coatesville, Pa.*, 1920.

Tempera, 19½ x 15½. Dr. and Mrs. William Carlos Williams.

his temperament was mocking, detached—and extraordinarily alert. Our country has produced many artists more powerful than he. It has produced none more rare in perception and control of vision.

Demuth: [Comparing his own and John Marin's debt to modern French art] *He brought his up in buckets and spilt much along the way. I dipped mine out with a teaspoon but I never spilled a drop.*

See: Andrew C. Ritchie, *Charles Demuth,* 1950. James Thrall Soby, *Contemporary American Painters,* 1948, pp. 9–15. S. Lane Faison, Jr., Fact and Art in Charles Demuth, *Magazine of Art,* Apr. 1950. pp. 123–127.

DEMUTH: *Poppies,* 1929.

Watercolor, 14 x 20. Mrs. Edith Gregor Halpert.

OPPOSITE:

DEMUTH: *I Saw The Figure 5 in Gold,* 1928.

Oil, 36 x 29¾. Metropolitan Museum of Art, bequest of Alfred Stieglitz.

CHARLES DEMUTH 55

LYONEL FEININGER

by Frederick S. Wight

LYONEL FEININGER lived in Europe for more than half a long life—fifty out of eighty years. Before the first World War he had already developed a geometric style for which cubism was at least an encouragement. But the source was quite personal. Feininger was trained to be a musician, and the formal music of Bach was the great influence upon him. Lines are organized like notes, and music allowed him to abstract from the accidental world of appearances.

He was born in New York in 1871. The first sixteen years of his life were spent in the New York region, and they have a particular importance, as his art is steeped in nostalgia and fed from early recollections. His parents were musicians, his father a violinist and composer, his mother a concert singer. They performed together and were often on tour. Solitude fed the boy's imagination, and New York developed his sense of wonder. There is a streak of fantasy, of Hans Christian Andersen in Feininger (he was a toymaker all his life) which offsets the severity of his dedication.

He followed his parents to Europe, joined them in Berlin, stayed on with his mother when they separated. After a period of indecision he gave up music for art school and emerged a caricaturist on *Lustige Blätter* and *Ulk*. He was in Paris working on *Le Temoin* by 1906. He ground through a year's contract to produce "funny papers" for the Chicago Tribune and brought this phase of his life to a conclusion.

FEININGER: *Locomotive with Big Wheel,* 1915.

Oil, 22⅛ x 47⅛. Estate of the artist.

FEININGER: *Bridge V*, 1919.

Oil, 31 x 39½. Philadelphia Museum of Art.

Determined to paint, he chose Zehlendorf in the suburbs of Berlin for his strenuous and private struggle toward a style of his own. Caricature—still showing in *Locomotive with Big Wheel*—had at least freed him from the literal. He was soon filling a congested space with brittle fragments of houses, bridges, and ships, and his canvases eventually became as abstract as *Bridges V*. Married, and with a family, he stayed on in Germany through the first World War.

He was the first artist chosen by the architect Walter Gropius for the staff of the school that became the Bauhaus. The 'twenties in Weimar and Dessau were great and expansive years for Feininger, working with Gropius, Kandinsky and Klee. His oils now took on depth, deep space filled with serenity and light, and the exalted romantic nature of his art came to the fore. Like Turner, he set the sun in the sky. Architecture on land or sea was his subject, but his lines—accord-

ing to Gropius—are not architecture, they are rays of light. So they must be straight, and must continue until they are reflected, or splinter off an opposing surface. Larger forms are luminous areas that shift like northern lights, while a few figures stand transfixed in the foreground, contemplating (in a mood of Goethe) a scene which is more a habitation for genius than the environment of men.

After the meager and then the evil times which followed, he left Germany like other men of good will. He taught at Mills College in 1936, and the following year he was home for good. He was unrecognized as an American, but his reputation, at first rescued by the discerning, gradually broadened its new base.

He lived in New York within walking distance of his

FEININGER: *Church of the Minorites, II*, 1926.

Oil, 47 x 43. Walker Art Center, Minneapolis.

FEININGER: *City at Night*, 1941.

Oil, 36 x 24. Wolf Collection.

birthplace, and the tall city served him well as subject matter. In his late years he turned more to water color, and an evening mist of atmosphere tended to blur his forms. But on occasion his talent blazed forth and he produced a number of conclusive works which have all his old-time authority and vigor.

He died in his native city, early in 1956.

Feininger: *In one respect, perhaps, my work may be considered of significance: Its passionate quest for strictest delineation of space, without any compromising. In the glaring sun these days, seconded by shadows cast on brilliantly lit surfaces I see motifs of colossal consequence. A perfectly new plane-space conception.* (From Letters to Julia, Curt Valentin Gallery, *Lyonel Feininger* exhibition catalogue, 1952.)

See: Museum of Modern Art, *Lyonel Feininger—Marsden Hartley* exhibition catalogue, ed. by Dorothy C. Miller, 1944, pp. 7–52. Institute of Contemporary Art, Boston, *Jacques Villon, Lyonel Feininger* exhibition catalogue, 1948, pp. 29–46. The Print Club of Cleveland and the Cleveland Museum of Art, *The Work of Lyonel Feininger* exhibition catalogue, 1951, pp. 5–46.

FEININGER:

Houses by the River, I, 1948.

Oil, 20 x 30. Collection Mrs. Windfor.

FEININGER: *Gelmeroda, VIII*, 1921.

Oil, 39¼ x 31¼. Whitney Museum of American Art.

JOSEPH STELLA

by John I. H. Baur

THE ONE outstanding futurist in America was Joseph Stella, although a number of other artists were influenced by this Italian-born movement which attempted to infuse dynamic motion into the static patterns of cubism in order to express the speed of contemporary life. Perhaps Stella's fascination with futurism was due in part to his Italian birth (at Muro Lucano in 1879 or '80—the date is still unsettled). Or it may be that his always romantic temperament found in the futurist style a perfect means to express his highly emotional response to New York. He had come here in 1896, had studied medicine for two years, then painting at the New York School of Art and Art Students League. For a time he was an illustrator and was sent by *The Survey* to draw Pittsburgh's steel mills. But Stella's mature career began when he met the Italian futurists on a trip to France and Italy in 1909–12, the years of the movement's birth. On his return he saw America with a new and typically futurist eye—a land of skyscrapers, clangor and rushing modernity. With furious intensity he set out to capture it on canvas.

First came his *Battle of Lights, Coney Island,* a painting full of the glitter and noise of its subject. Taking elements from all parts of the amusement park, breaking them into fragments, reassembling them in a wildly gyrating pattern of futurist V-lines and curving force lines, Stella showed a natural mastery of the futurist method. All of this skill and even more feeling went into his painting of *Brooklyn Bridge,* a subject that obsessed him as "the shrine containing all the efforts of the new civilization of America," and which moved him as if "in the presence of a new DIVINITY." Seldom has a feat of engineering been more romantically celebrated than in the night vision of the bridge which he painted, according to his notes, "rapid and

STELLA: *Spring,* 1914.

Oil, 75 x 40⅛. Yale University Art Gallery, Collection Société Anonyme.

OPPOSITE:

STELLA:

Battle of Lights, Coney Island, 1913.

Oil, 75¾ x 84. Yale University Art Gallery, Collection Société Anonyme.

JOSEPH STELLA   63

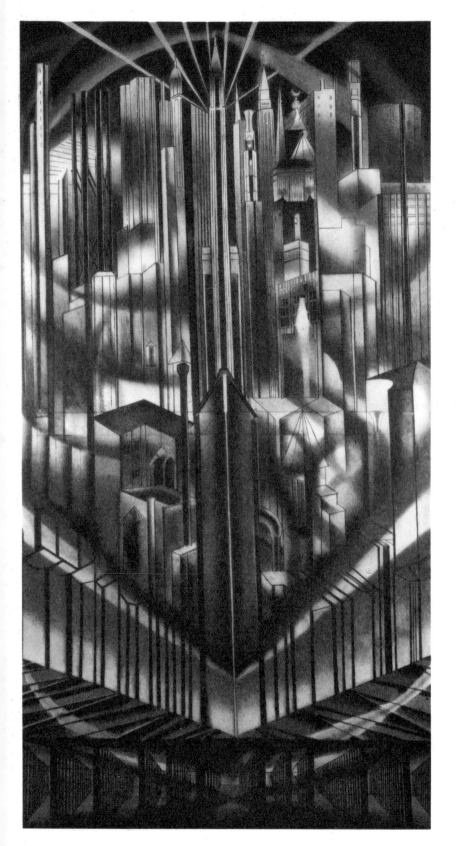

intense with no effort." Stella's final apotheosis of the metropolis was the set of five immense panels called *New York Interpreted,* done in 1920–22. A little drier and more labored than his earlier work, they are nevertheless a vivid synthesis of the city's soaring aspects, its total impact on the senses.

Stella lived until 1946 but the last twenty-five years of his life produced little of consequence. From the beginning he had been drawn to nature as well as to the machine age, and occasionally he had used his futurist method, as in the picture *Spring,* to weave a poetic pattern of growth. More often, however, his nature subjects were done in a decorative style of over-bright colors that has not worn well. It is for his ardent response to New York that Stella will be best remembered.

Stella: *And when in 1912 I came back to New York I was thrilled to find America so rich with so many new motives to be translated into a new art.*

Steel and electricity had created a new world. A new drama had surged . . . a new poliphony was ringing all around with the scintillating, highly-colored lights. The steel had leaped to hyperbolic altitudes and expanded to vast latitudes with the skyscrapers and with bridges made for the conjunction of worlds. A new architecture was created, a new perspective. (From *Autobiographical Notes,* below.)

See: Joseph Stella, *Autobiographical Notes,* unpublished ms., Whitney Museum of American Art. Newark Museum, *Joseph Stella* exhibition catalogue, introd. by Arthur F. Egener, 1939. Stella number, *The Little Review,* Autumn, 1922.

MAX WEBER *by Lloyd Goodrich*

MAX WEBER, born in Russia in 1881, was brought up in the deeply religious culture of Russian Judaism. Coming to America at ten, he struggled through poverty to achieve an education in art. In 1905 he went abroad for three years, and in Paris came in direct contact with the beginnings of the modern movement and knew many of its leaders. On his return to America he became one of the earliest pioneers of modernism, with all the hardships that this involved.

Weber's earliest work was allied to the exuberant paganism of the fauves. But in 1912 he began experiments in abstraction, notably a series of compositions based on New York. Unlike the naturalistic genre of the Henri group, these were free interpretations of the city's dynamism, its energy, movement and color. With parallels to both cubism and futurism, they were more emotional and expressionist, especially in their color, deep and rich rather than brilliant, and in their vital, sensitive graphic quality. In these years Weber was one of the earliest exponents of abstract art in any country, and its most inventive exponent in America. But temperamentally he was (and still is) opposed to pure or formal abstraction.

One of the deepest sources of Weber's art has been his Jewish heritage—that long history so rich in spiritual genius. His fundamentally religious nature began to express itself in his painting during his middle thirties. A mystical note, clear and strong in themes of prayer and contemplation, also pervaded other subjects not obviously religious. His idyllic scenes of women singing and playing instruments had a biblical character that recalled *The Song of Songs*. His style, abandoning abstract tendencies, became representational and classic; his women were monumental in the heavy, maternal richness of their bodies.

When Weber was approaching sixty his art began to display a growing imaginative fantasy and freedom of style. In certain subjects there was an intensification of Jewish character, as in his Hebrew scholars meditating and discussing. At the same time came a trend toward abstraction, though never again reaching the purely abstract. Objects remained recognizable, but were now used as springboards for plastic invention. Figures were translated into forms remarkable for their expressive power, their eloquent distortion, their intensity of life. Line took on an independent existence,

WEBER: *The Geranium,* 1911.

Oil, 39⅞ x 32¼. Museum of Modern Art.

WEBER: *Three Literary Gentlemen*, 1945.
Oil, 29 x 36. Collection William H. Lane Foundation.

WEBER: *Chinese Restaurant*, 1915.

Oil, 40 x 48. Whitney Museum of American Art.

achieving linear patterns alive with movement and rhythm. Sensitive, vibrating, charged with feeling, it was the violin in the orchestration of the design. His color remained deep-toned; few painters know so well how to use black to give depth to their color, or by contrast, value to the higher notes. But in recent years a flowering of his palette has brought new hues and deliberate dissonances, again proving him one of the most gifted colorists of today. His work of the past decade, based on an accumulated richness of artistry, reveals Weber as one of the foremost contemporary artists achieving intense emotional expression in the language of plastic design.

Weber: *In the infinite beauty and revelation of nature, and in the inherent spiritual and cultural values of humanity, I find a universe of inspiring motifs for aesthetic plastic interpretation.*

To safeguard against alluring pitfalls of obscurantism, I eschew vague idiom, false inference, geometric calligraphic maze and color-blind pigmentation.

For inspiration and incentive, I reflect upon the concept and vision, the grandeur and austerity of the great ancients of all races and climes. Their legacy is as modern and living as it is ancient and eternal.

In carrying on my own humble creative effort, I depend greatly upon that which I do not yet know, and upon that which I have not yet done.

See: Holger Cahill, *Max Weber,* 1930. Lloyd Goodrich, *Max Weber,* 1949.

WEBER: *Tranquility*, 1928.

Oil, 32 x 40⅛. The artist.

WEBER:

Hasidic Dance, 1940.

Oil, 32 x 40. Mr. and Mrs. Milton Lowenthal.

WEBER: *Adoration of the Moon, 1944.*

Oil, 48⅛ x 31⅞. Whitney Museum of American Art.

MARSDEN HARTLEY

by Frederick S. Wight

MARSDEN HARTLEY had a great and late triumph: in his last decade he forged a life's work into a unified whole. It was combined from elements unusually discordant and contradictory, even for our times, and the tensions mastered and controlled are the driving force in his work. Superficially he was an artist caught in the nineteenth-century dilemma, the choice between the European tradition and the American adventure. He travelled widely, endlessly; it was half search, half flight. He was caught between gregariousness and need of solitude, between paint and a desire to write, between sophisticated sensibilities and respect for the far simpler people from whom he came. He came home from his migrations to his native Maine, his world-education matured, able to build such paintings as *The Wave* or *Mt. Katahdin*—on bedrock, out of the Maine elementals of water, rock, sea and sky.

He seems to have been faced by some deeper, Whitmanesque choice of loving either himself or humanity as a whole, and he achieved a synthesis even here in paintings such as *The Lost Felice* or *Fishermen's Last Supper,* which are religious events.

Hartley was born in Lewiston, Maine, in 1877, spent his later boyhood in Ohio, came to study art in New York (with Chase among others) and was back in Maine by 1901. The "black paintings" with which he began were influenced by the American painter-mystic, Albert Pinkham Ryder, whose massive glacial clouds were to stay for good in Hartley's skies. Stieglitz, the impresario of the new, showed Hartley in New York in 1909; three years later he and Arthur B. Davies (of Armory Show fame) combined to send Hartley to Europe. The painter met Gertrude Stein and saw the new world of cubism in Paris, but he elected to go to Munich and join Franz Marc. Bold patterns built out of literary symbolism now related his work to the Blue Rider Group; he stayed on in Berlin into the first World War.

HARTLEY:

Portrait of Albert Pinkham Ryder, 1938–39.

Oil, 28 x 22. Mr. and Mrs. Milton Lowenthal.

OPPOSITE:

HARTLEY: *Mt. Katahdin, Autumn, No. 1,* 1939–40.

Oil, 30⅛ x 40. F. M. Hall Collection, University of Nebraska Art Galleries.

HARTLEY: *The Wave,* 1940.

Oil, 30½ x 41. Worcester Museum of Art.

OPPOSITE:

HARTLEY: *Fishermen's Last Supper,* 1940–41.

Oil, 29⅞ x 41. Mr. and Mrs. Roy S. Neuberger.

HARTLEY: *Portrait of a German Officer,* 1914.

Oil, 68¼ x 41⅜. Alfred Stieglitz Collection, Metropolitan Museum of Art.

He returned to New England, then explored the West —his European patterns becoming something as American as a Navaho blanket with astonishingly little change. More than a decade of restless travel began. Berlin again, Paris, the South of France where he felt the influence of Cézanne and brought a new discipline and severity into his work. Then London, America again, Mexico, and once more Berlin. Betweenwhiles New England persisted as a center of gravity and strengthened its hold upon him. He explored the coast from Gloucester to Nova Scotia, and for the last ten years settled, like Marin, for alternations of Maine and New York: the metropolis in the winter, Bangor in the summer.

His style, as it came into the clear, was both linear and massive, diagrammatic, austere, and consciously crude. His subjects: landscapes, still lifes, and a couple of portraits of presiding geniuses—Albert Pinkham Ryder and Abraham Lincoln. The painting is bleak and arctic even when the color is strong. Curiously, dropping the emotional temperature seems to have permitted Hartley a release of power.

HARTLEY: *Wild Roses,* 1942.

Oil, 22 x 28. Phillips Collection, Washington.

Hartley: *My feeling is: of what use is a painting which does not realize its esthetical problem? Underlying all sensible works of art, there must be somewhere in evidence the particular problem understood. It was so with those artists of the great past who had the intellectual knowledge of structure upon which to place their emotions. It is this structural beauty that makes the old painting valuable. And so it becomes to me—a problem. I would rather be sure that I had placed two colors in true relationship to each other than to have exposed a wealth of emotionalism gone wrong in the name of richness of personal expression.* (From Museum of Modern Art catalogue below.)

See: Museum of Modern Art, *Lyonel Feininger—Marsden Hartley* exhibition catalogue, ed. by Monroe Wheeler, 1944, pp. 54–96. D. Gallup, Weaving a Pattern, Gertrude Stein and Marsden Hartley, *Magazine of Art,* Nov. 1948, pp. 156–161. Elizabeth McCausland, Return of the Native: Marsden Hartley, *Art in America,* Spring 1952, pp. 55–79.

ARTHUR G. DOVE

by John I. H. Baur

AS EARLY AS 1906 Arthur Dove was a successful illustrator, earning the then comfortable income of $4,000 a year. Six years later he had put illustrating behind him to devote his full energies to those mysteriously evocative graphs of sun and moon power, of farm and sea shapes, which have finally won him recognition as perhaps the most individual of our pioneer abstractionists. Unfortunately that recognition did not become general soon enough to bring much comfort to a life of hardship that ended at Centerport, Long Island, in 1946.

Dove was born at Canandaigua, N. Y., in 1880 and was brought up in nearby Geneva. At Cornell, from which he graduated in 1903, he did some painting under Charles Furlong of the art department, then went to New York, married, had a son and was soon established in commercial art. The turning point in his career was an eighteen-month trip to France in 1907–08, a time when the modern fauve and cubist movements were just making their first stir. Dove was deeply influenced and soon began a series of semi-abstract pastels symbolizing growth patterns in nature or "the creak and strain," as one critic put it, of a *Team of Horses*. In 1912 a group of these pictures were shown by Alfred Stieglitz in Dove's first one-man exhibition, which also travelled to Chicago, causing a fist fight among visiting art students.

Dove's decision to give up commercial work caused a long rift with his father, who refused to give him even a small allowance. For the next six years Dove ran a chicken farm at Westport, Connecticut, lobstering on the side and working from four in the morning till midnight. In 1918 he gave up the farm, acquired a boat and lived up and down the Hudson River and the Long Island coast, spending some of his later years ashore at Port Washington, Lloyd's Harbor and Huntington. After his mother's death in 1933, he sold the boat and returned to Geneva to help salvage what he could of the family's dwindling finances. There the Doves (he had remarried in 1923 after his first wife's death) lived four years on an old farm and two more in an abandoned rollerskating rink. There, too, he was stricken with the heart ailment that made him a semi-invalid for the rest of his life. His last years were spent on Long Island, first at Halesite then at Centerport where he remodelled an old post office, its rear supported on piers over the salt water which he loved.

Through this harried life, Dove's art developed slowly but with remarkable consistency. Soon he abandoned the almost geometrical forms of his early abstractions, moving in the 1920's towards more fluid, sweeping lines. Perhaps the rhythm of these seemed a little obvious, for he went on in his mature work to a style of strange, ragged shapes, each one carefully wrought to express the essence of his subjects. They are entirely original. Who but Dove would have visualized the sound of fog horns in wavering, expanding circles or have perched the moon like a female symbol above a phallic tree? In his late work he evolved more abstract forms, which have had a strong influence on several of our younger painters, but he never surpassed his haunting nature poetry of the 'thirties.

Dove: *As I see from one point in space to another, from the top of the tree to the top of the sun, from right or left, or up, or down, these are drawn as any line around a thing to give the colored stuff of it, to weave the whole into a sequence of formations rather than to form an arrangement of facts.* (From An American Place, Arthur G. Dove exhibition catalogue, 1940.)

See: Elizabeth McCausland, Dove, Man and Painter, *Parnassus,* Dec. 1937, pp. 3–6. Duncan Phillips, Arthur G. Dove, 1880–1946, *Magazine of Art,* May 1947, pp. 193–7. Suzanne M. Mullett, *Arthur G. Dove,* 1944 (unpublished Master's Thesis, The American University).

DOVE: *Moon,* 1935.

Oil, 35 x 27. Mr. and Mrs. M. M. Zurier.

DOVE: *Team of Horses*, 1912.

Pastel. 18½ x 21½. Dr. Mary B. Holt.

DOVE:

Fog Horns, 1929.

Oil, 19 x 27.
Colorado Springs
Fine Arts Center.

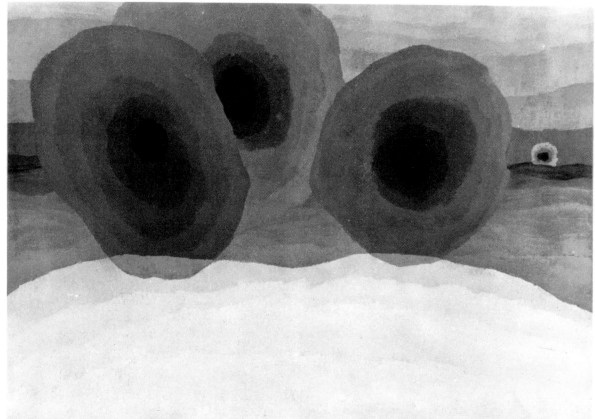

82

DOVE: *Cow at Play,* 1940.

Oil, 20 x 30. Permanent Collection, Fine Arts Department, International Business Machines Corp.

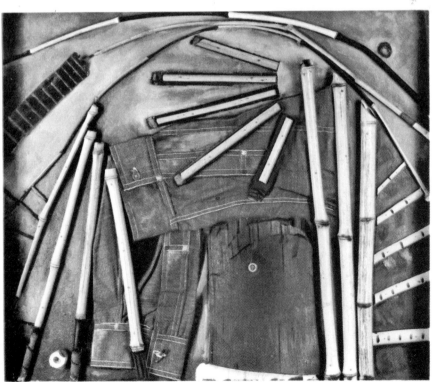

DOVE: *Goin' Fishin',* ca. 1925.

Collage, 19½ x 14. Phillips Collection, Washington.

STANTON MACDONALD-WRIGHT

by John I. H. Baur

MACDONALD-WRIGHT:

"Conception" Synchromy, ca. 1915.

Oil, 30 x 24. Whitney Museum of American Art.

ONE OF THE militant vanguard of American abstract painters in the early years of the century was the young Stanton Macdonald-Wright who, with his friend Morgan Russell, founded the Synchromist movement. Born in Charlottesville, Virginia, on July 8, 1890, Macdonald-Wright began to study art when he was only seven. In 1900 he moved to California where he was educated in public and private schools as well as by tutors. At seventeen he went abroad for the first time, living principally in Paris and Cassis, France. During his first four months in the French capital he managed to attend thirteen different art schools, finally settling down at the Ecole des Beaux Arts and the Sorbonne. Michelangelo and Cézanne were his favorite painters at this time, but soon he was deeply impressed by the work of the cubists, which was first shown in Paris in 1908. By 1912 he and Russell were also doing abstract and semi-abstract work, called "synchromies," which they exhibited at the Carrol Gallery in New York in 1913, then in Munich and at Bernheim-Jeune's in Paris later the same year.

Synchromism owed a heavy debt to cubism but the young Americans sought to remake that movement in terms of deep space and dynamic motion. To do this they used the brilliant colors of the spectrum, which seem to recede or advance according to their arrangement and hue. Handled with great sensitivity by Macdonald-Wright, the effect is somewhat like that of a brilliant and constantly shifting kaleidoscope. At almost precisely the same time, a group of French artists

MACDONALD-WRIGHT: *Oriental: Synchromy in Blue-Green*, 1918. Oil, 36 x 50. Whitney Museum of American Art.

known as the Orphists were working in a similar vein. With them the Americans waged a spirited battle of manifestoes, even challenging Delaunay, their leader, to hang his best painting in their Bernheim-Jeune exhibition so that the public could judge the respective merits of the two movements. Actually neither Orphism nor Synchromism lasted long or attracted many followers, but both were important steps in the rapid growth of abstract art.

Macdonald-Wright, himself, gave up Synchromism about 1919 and went to study in California and later in the far east. He did not exhibit again until 1932, and since then his work has frequently changed direction. For many years he has taught Oriental and modern art at the University of California at Los Angeles.

Macdonald-Wright: *Every color has its own position in emotional space and possesses a well defined character. I conceive of space itself as endowed with plastic meaning, expressed through color. Since form is not the volume of each object seen separately, I organized my canvas as a whole, as much in depth as on the surface . . . With us the quality of depth provokes a subjective emotion.* (From the catalogue below.)

See: Bernheim-Jeune & Cie, *Les Synchromistes Morgan Russell et S. Macdonald-Wright* exhibition catalogue, 1913.

MACDONALD-WRIGHT:

Airplane Synchromy in Yellow and Orange, c. 1917.

Oil, 24¼ x 24¼. Alfred Stieglitz Collection, Philadelphia Museum of Art.

MAN RAY

by James Thrall Soby

"HE [THE ARTIST] uncovers the pure plane of expression that has so long been hidden by the glazings of nature imitation, anecdote and other popular subjects." In these words, written for the Forum Exhibition of 1916 at the Anderson Galleries in New York, Man Ray announced his participation in the revolt against naturalism in art which had begun with the postimpressionists and continued in more extreme form with the cubists and abstractionists. He was one of the first —and most fervent—of American painters to join the struggle against the old traditions of realism and storytelling.

Born in Philadelphia in 1890, Man Ray had been trained as an architect and engineer before deciding to become a painter. Like many of his insurrectionary compatriots, he was stirred by the Armory Show of 1913. After that famous event, his art became more and more abstract. But Man Ray's closest affinity was with those painters who brought to abstraction a sense of ironic mockery, quite different from cubism's unyielding solemnity. He was associated with Marcel Duchamp and Francis Picabia in the short-lived but brilliant New York Dada movement during World War I; his *Rope Dancer Accompanies Herself with Her Shadows* is one of the movement's most memorable images.

From the mid-1920's on, Man Ray was an active member of surrealism's inner circle in Paris, working as a painter and also, with growing absorption, as a photographer. In photography he flatly rejected the premise of truth-to-medium urged by many of his colleagues. He felt free to manipulate both negatives and prints in any way that suited his purpose—enlarging, cropping, distorting, solarizing, etc. The result was a remarkable series of quite abstract photographic prints known as "rayographs" and a number of the most revealing portraits of our era.

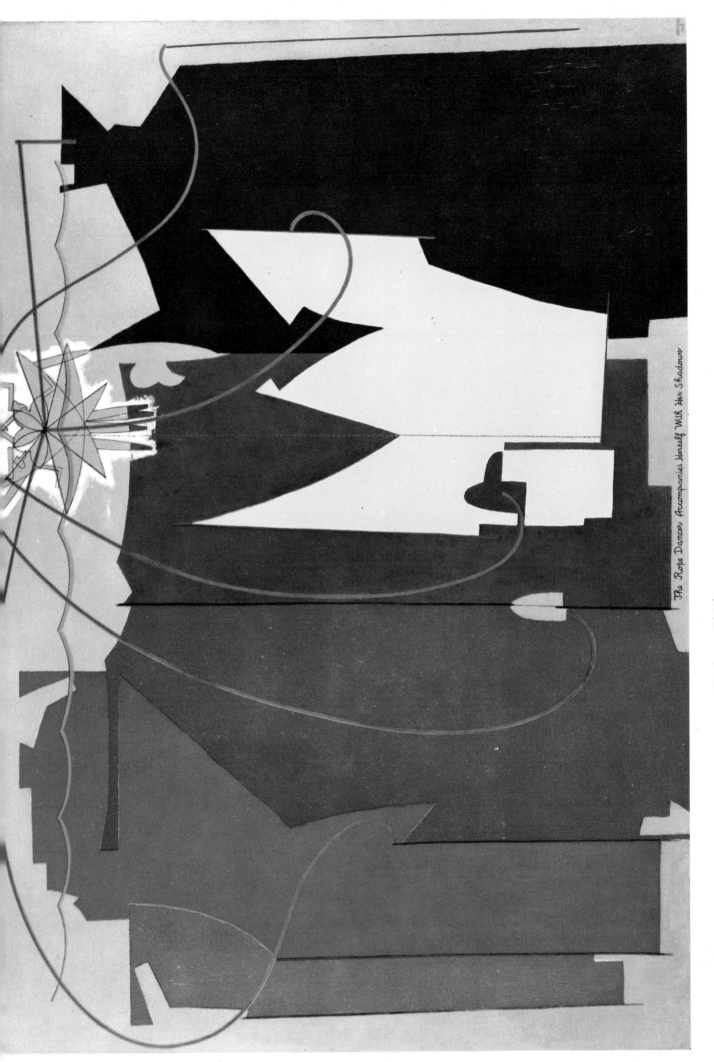

The Rope Dancer Accompanies Herself With Her Shadows

RAY: *The Rope Dancer Accompanies Herself with Her Shadows*, 1916. Oil, 52 x 73⅜. Museum of Modern Art.

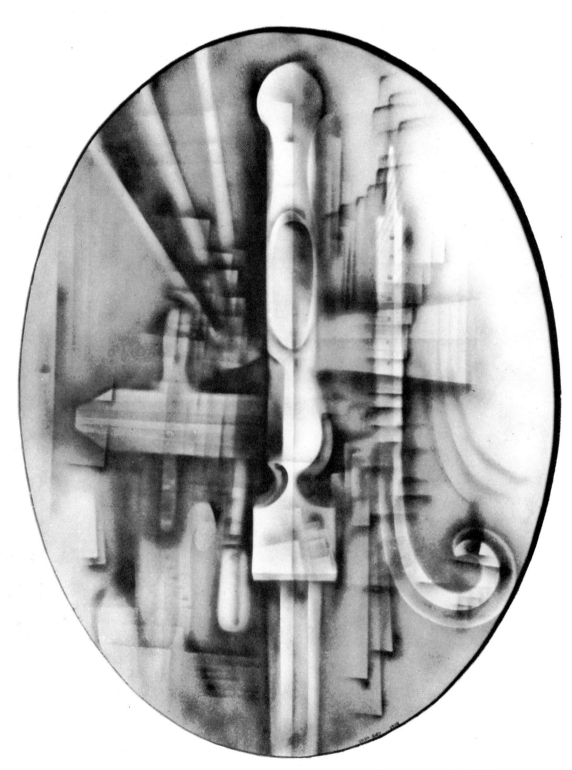

RAY: *Aerograph*, 1919.

Airbrush and watercolor, 27 x 20. The artist.

Ray: *I have no particular aims or beliefs about painting. If at times I have been associated with various schools, it is simply because my work at the time seemed to run a parallel course. And I have always accepted and been flattered by unconditional invitations, whatever the school.*

Pleasure and the pursuit of liberty are the guiding motives of my work.

I do not know what is good or bad in painting as neither has ever hurt me nor anyone else. There are plenty of self-appointed specialists to decide this question. If I must choose between being original or being profound, I certainly prefer originality. I believe that if I am so built, the most superficial effort I make will have meaning; and if I am basically superficial, all my efforts at significance will be of no avail. Again I prefer to leave the decision to others.

Oh yes, there is another motive: I consider all creative work an escape from the competitive life. This is what distinguishes us from the rest of nature.

I could go on and fill a book, but for the time being I am painting, so if you are interested, try and look at my paintings.

See: Man Ray, *Alphabet for Adults*, Copley Galleries, Beverly Hills, c. 1948. Robert Motherwell, *The Dada Painters and Poets*, 1951. Robert Desnos, The Work of Man Ray, *Transition*, Feb. 1929, pp. 264–266. Georges Tibemont-Dessaignes, *Man Ray*, Gallimard, Paris, 1924.

RAY: *The Taming of the Shrew*, 1948.

Oil, 20 x 16. Mr. and Mrs. Albert Lewin.

MAN RAY   91

THE
NATIVE SCENE

1920-1940

Sheeler

Spencer

O'Keeffe

Evergood

Shahn

Levine

Benton

Wood

Kane

Hopper

Burchfield

Kuniyoshi

Grosz

Watkins

Lebrun

Maurer

Davis

Gorky

Tobey

Albright

Blume

Pickens

Dickinson

THE YEAR 1920 may be taken as a turning point in American art. Many of the social realists, who had pioneered in the discovery of the city, turned at about this time to other interests, particularly to esthetic problems which had little to do with the spontaneous genre painting of their youth. Glackens fell in love with Renoir and became an impressionist. Bellows was absorbed by Jay Hambidge's theory of Dynamic Symmetry. Even Sloan, who remained most faithful to the group's original aims, began to paint more landscapes and nudes and to experiment with glazing and cross hatching. Some of the old enthusiasm and excitement had gone.

At exactly the same time, most of our early modernists turned back in a more conservative direction. Macdonald-Wright gave up Synchromism. Weber and Hartley abandoned abstraction for their individual forms of expressionism. The work of both Dove and Feininger became more naturalistic. It was far from a total retreat, but it was a marked adjustment between their youthful rebellion and the main current of American art. Such a reaction might well have taken place even without the hostile attitude of our critics and public, for no artist can escape entirely from the cultural climate in which he has been raised. Virtually all of the American modernists seem to have felt a compulsion to relate their early experiments to native tradition. If this was a compromise, it was generally a productive one, and produced some notable work. Even when it did not immediately do so, as with Marsden Hartley, it was apparently a necessary preparation for a final flowering that came later.

The most important single development in American art during the 1920's was the birth of the precisionist or Immaculate movement, and this, too, was the fruit of just such a compromise. One of the principles of modern art which appealed particularly to Americans was that the design of a picture must function with the absolute precision of a machine. Since the machine was already accepted as a peculiarly American symbol, it is not strange that a number of our artists—led by Demuth, Sheeler and Niles Spencer—were drawn to paint it in a precise, sharp-edged, hard-surfaced style that was itself machine-like in character. Using extreme simplifications, learned from cubism and futurism, these artists, and the many younger ones who soon joined them, brought their semi-abstract designs into an appropriate and easily understood relation to their subjects. The latter included factories, bridges, ships, grain elevators, Shaker architecture and, in general, those forms that combined functional simplicity with a distinctively native character. Immaculate art was a little chilly—despite the fact that Georgia O'Keeffe turned it into a more personal vehicle of expression—and it did not, as a movement, survive much beyond the 1920's. But it was the first widespread, truly popular compromise between American realism and international abstraction, and its influence is still felt in our art today. Its decline in the early 1930's was due less, one suspects, to any lack of vitality in the style itself than it was to the economic depression which shadowed those years and made us not quite so complacent with our machine-made, industrial civilization.

The depression had a more profound, or at least a more demonstrable, effect on American art than any other external event of the decade. In a country which had always considered art a luxury, the painter was one of the first to suffer. He was also one of the first to question the justice of a social order that seemed to have dealt the worst hardship to those who were least responsible for the situation. The result was the rapid growth of a school of "social protest," or "socially conscious," painting which attacked wealth and privilege and allied itself with the worker, the jobless, the racial minorities. Members of this group were more closely knit than those in most American art movements. Their bond was a passionate conviction that art must justify itself by its service to humanity, that the artist must become a responsible member of society, indeed that he had a special obligation to be society's conscience. Abstract art, in their view, was a retreat from reality, an experiment in an ivory tower. Yet the social protest painters were more advanced stylistically than many of their contemporaries. All of them made free use of expressionist distortion, often pushed to violent extremes. This was not quite the same as being orthodox expressionists, for the latter used distortion, regardless of subject, to express a constantly romantic attitude towards life. In the hands of the social protest painters, distortion served a more restricted purpose; it was a weapon of attack, a tool to dramatize a specific situation. At times social protest art was rather declamatory, but in the work of its best men, such as Ben Shahn, Philip Evergood and Jack Levine, it reached a moving sincerity and a perfect adjustment of means to end.

In one sense the socially conscious painters were the artistic descendants of Sloan, Bellows and the other pioneers in urban genre. At least they concerned themselves with events in the lives of real people, caught in familiar settings and circumstances. On a wider scale, and without the ingredient of angry protest, this revival of interest in contemporary life became a dominant trend in our art from late in the 1920 s to at least 1940. It has often been suggested that the popularity of American Scene painting was closely related to a wave of nationalism (and in some quarters isolationism) which swept the country after the first World War. But nationalism is a broad word. So far as the arts are concerned, it generally means regionalism, since every man's concept of his native land is based on his limited experience of certain parts and certain people. It is not surprising, then, that many different groups sprang up and that they explored different aspects of America with quite different attitudes. The most militant regionalism was that of a middle-western group led by Thomas Benton, Grant Wood and John Steuart Curry—the famous "Triumvirate" of the 1930's. Espousing realism in various forms, they produced some still memorable pictures of rural and small-town America, but they also expended a good deal of energy attacking "decadent" European art and even the "effete" creations of the eastern seaboard. In the long run their program, always a rather self-conscious one, became a straight-jacket for their painting. The best of the regionalists, indeed, were men like Edward Hopper and Charles Burchfield who never thought of themselves in that term and belonged to no group but who were drawn by deep compassion to record the kind of American life they knew.

Regionalism is generally associated with the widespread return to realism that occurred in these years. The two did indeed go hand in hand, but they were not synonymous. Among the expressionists, Marin's scenes of the Maine coast and of lower New York were plainly inspired by his profound attachment to those places. Even some abstract work, especially that of Dove and Stuart Davis, was based on a response to distinctively American subjects and bore the stamp of specific time and place.

In spite of the general reaction against modernism during this period, a number of painters, in addition to those mentioned above, continued to work in an abstract or expressionist vein. On the whole their art was more international than regional in character and incorporated a variety of influences from abroad. George Grosz brought a strain of German mysticism with him when he settled in America in 1932. Yasuo Kuniyoshi and Mark Tobey were both deeply affected by oriental art, Arshile Gorky by his recollections of the Sumerian culture of Armenia, where he was born. Many, like Maurer, had lived and studied for years in Paris. These men, with others, swam counter to the American Scene current and kept alive a concern with the cosmopolitan, formal trends in 20th-century painting.

A quite different modern movement, surrealism, also reached America in the early 1930's and soon affected a number of our painters. Founded in France in 1924, surrealism claimed the subconscious as its province; its subjects were dreams, hallucinations and those hidden impulses which lie deep in the atavistic layers of the mind. The strict surrealist did not believe in consciously designing a picture, but rather in letting the mind's image grow unprompted on the canvas. It followed that surrealism was even more opposed to cubist and expressionist art (since these were strongly designed) than it was to conservative, academic realism—which indeed it often resembled in technique. Surrealism eventually developed its own kind of abstraction, but in the 1930's

its meticulously realistic branch was the one which had the greatest influence here. Even so, relatively few Americans embraced it wholeheartedly. Man Ray, living in Paris, was perhaps closest to the French group. More typical was the varying reaction of men like Ivan Albright, Peter Blume, Edwin Dickinson and Alton Pickens. These painters emulated surrealism's immensely skillful technique and they followed its path into a realm of fantasy, but they did not give up all concern with design and their fantasy tended to be either more poetic or more closely linked to common experience than that of the wilder dreamers abroad.

As the decade of the 1930's ended in the second World War, American art came to another major turning point. The next few years saw a dramatic revival of abstract art and, with it, a strong reaction against our regional painting of the 1920's and '30's. To many critics and artists, that regionalism began to seem chauvinistic in subject and creatively bankrupt in its various forms of naturalism. A fairer estimate would acknowledge that these were its common pitfalls, which it did not always escape, but that regionalism at its best, and in its largest sense, produced a moving art rooted in a deep emotional response to America.

CHARLES SHEELER

by Frederick S. Wight

THE AMERICAN WAY of seeing rather than the American scene is Charles Sheeler's contribution. Faith in things, in industry and invention, has cleared away the irrelevance of atmosphere. Intent on abstract order, he finds it in the work of man's hands. He carries the industrial scene back to the clarity of the blueprint, the utensil back to the bench. In the end he has painted a sort of pragmatic faith in private effort: what the American really means by the word capitalism.

He was born in Philadelphia in 1883; studied at the School of Industrial Art, then at the Pennsylvania Academy under William Chase. He saw Europe in Chase's entourage, took a number of years to free himself from Chase's bravura brushwork and the one-time attack. A further trip to Europe in 1909 proved a voyage of discovery. Italy disclosed a new world of form in Giotto and Piero della Francesca; in Paris Sheeler opened his eyes to Cézanne, Renoir, and above all to the early cubism of Picasso. He came home with a new conception of paint.

He took up photography for self-support and developed it into an art which complemented his painting, a front rank accomplishment in itself. He became a photographer for architects. Weekends, in Doylestown, he experimented with cubism and his painting reflected an architectural bent. He found subject matter in the sober early buildings of the region.

He exhibited in the Armory Show, and in the first Independents, when he met the Walter Arensbergs, who introduced him into an advanced experimental group in New York. There he worked with Edward Steichen on *Vogue*.

A commission to photograph the Ford plant at River Rouge turned Sheeler to the industrial scene. A few years of crystallization were needed before it emerged in paint. *Upper Deck* set a pattern in 1929; in the early

thirties *Classic Landscape* recalled Detroit. In industry and invention, the painter saw an abstraction built of the forces of nature. He saw integrity invested in our constructions. This was what America meant.

His paintings of the early American scene, begun in Doylestown, have continued to parallel the transcriptions of industry. But Sheeler was not painting for the record. He was responding to the same thing which he saw in Detroit—integrity, function; and when he paints *Americana, Shaker Buildings, Kitchen, Williams-*

SHEELER: *Church Street El*, 1919.

Oil, 18½ x 15½. Mrs. Earle Horter.

SHEELER: *Upper Deck,* 1929.

Oil, 29⅛ x 22⅛. Fogg Art Museum.

burg, it is the integrity he gives us, behind the artifacts, utensils and houses. These things look as they do because they too were seriously meant.

The 1940's saw a change. Color was now for intensity instead of for clarification. Forms took on a complex life of their own, overlaying each other, composing in a sort of counterpoint. The painter no longer accepts abstraction made at the factory; he takes a hand in the inventive process, reaches onto the drawing board, asks us to tell time from the back of the watch.

Sheeler: *I can't go out and find something to paint. Something keeps recurring in memory with an insistence increasingly vivid and with attributes added which escape observation on first acquaintance. Gradually a mental image is built up which takes on a personal identity. The picture takes on a mental existence that is complete within the limits of my capacities, before the actual work of putting it down begins. Since the value of the mental picture can be determined only by the degree of response it arouses in other persons it must be re-stated in physical terms—hence the painting.* (From Constance Rourke, *Charles Sheeler,* 1938.)

See: Constance Rourke, *Charles Sheeler, Artist in the American Tradition,* 1938. Museum of Modern Art, *Charles Sheeler, Paintings, Drawings, Photographs; with an introduction by William Carlos Williams,* exhibition catalogue, 1939. Art Galleries, University of California, Los Angeles, *Charles Sheeler, a Retrospective Exhibition* catalogue with essays by William Carlos Williams, Bartlett H. Hayes, Jr., Frederick S. Wight, 1954.

OPPOSITE:

SHEELER: *Americana,* 1931.

Oil, 48 x 36. Mr. and Mrs. Milton Lowenthal.

98   CHARLES SHEELER

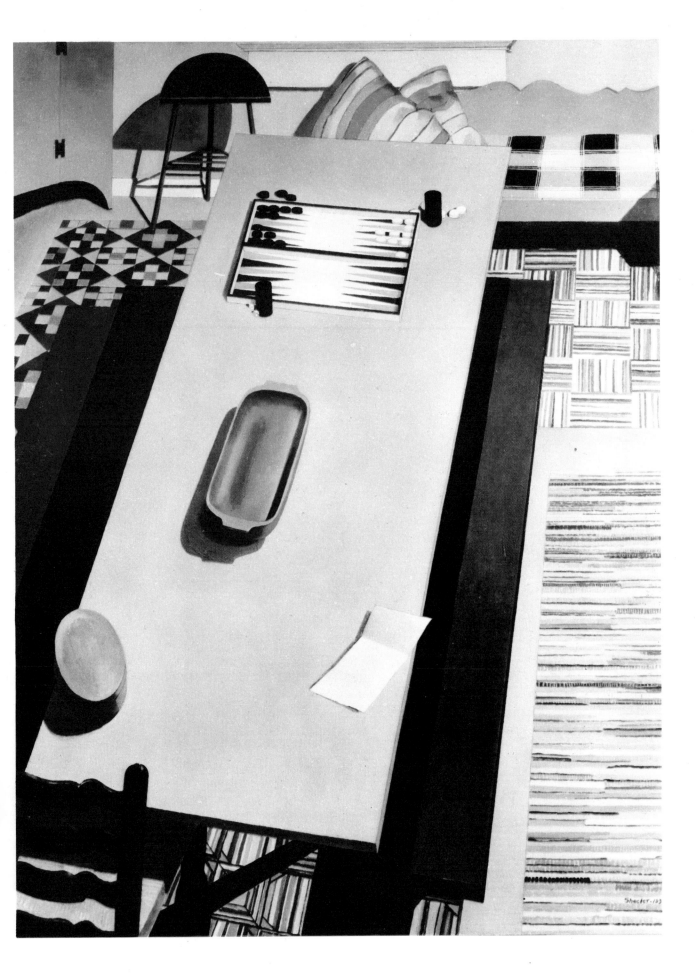

SHEELER: *Architectural Cadences*, 1954.
Oil, 25 x 35. Whitney Museum of American Art.

NILES SPENCER *by Dorothy C. Miller*

NILES SPENCER'S work came to maturity in the early 1920's. Born of Yankee stock in Pawtucket, Rhode Island, he found in the old seacoast towns of Maine and Cape Cod a favorite theme for his early work. His most characteristic subject, however, was to be the urban scene, the factories, skyscrapers, bridges, warehouses and dwellings of the city, which his quietly searching, intense vision distilled in precisely simplified forms. From the beginning he loved New York, and it was the abstract pattern of the city rather than the life of its inhabitants that moved him. His unpeopled canvases have the strength of understatement, a feeling for design that is both sensitive and profound, and a muted poetry of color.

Spencer was born in 1893 and studied from 1913 to 1915 at the Rhode Island School of Design, Providence. During a brief stay in New York in 1915 he studied with Bellows and Henri at the Ferrer School, and the following year he went to New York to live. Summers, and a number of winters as well, were spent on the coast of Maine at Ogunquit, where he lived in the artists' colony at Perkins Cove started by Hamilton Easter Field.

In 1921–22 and again in 1928–29 Spencer lived in France and Italy. In 1923 he joined the Whitney Studio Club and showed there till 1930. Two one-man shows in 1925 and 1928 won him recognition and a firm place in American art, though he did not hold another one-man show until 1947. A commission from the Section of Fine Arts of the Treasury Department for a mural for the post office at Aliquippa, Pennsylvania, was completed in 1937. His paintings are owned by major museums throughout the U.S.A.

SPENCER: *City Walls, 1921.*

Oil, 39⅜ x 28¾. Museum of Modern Art.

SPENCER: *In Fairmont,* 1951.

Oil, 65½ x 41½. Museum of Modern Art.

SPENCER:

The Cove, Ogunquit, 1922.

Oil, 28¼ x 36. Newark Museum.

SPENCER:

The Green Table, 1930.

Oil, 50 x 40. Whitney Museum of American Art.

From 1923 till about 1940 Spencer divided his time between Provincetown, Massachusetts and New York, where he lived in the old Washington Square section he painted so often. After 1940 he made New York his permanent home, but again sought out an old seacoast town, Sag Harbor, Long Island, for the summers.

Spencer's untimely death in 1952 interrupted a powerful series of canvases devoted to the theme of industrial America, paintings increasingly abstract in feeling though they never lost their frame of reference in nature.

Spencer: *The winters at Ogunquit [in the early 1920's] came as a revelation. I had more or less expected bleakness, cold and lonely isolation, but the actuality was quite different. The storms, the clear cold sunlight and especially the quiet silvery gray days when the sea, sky and land achieved a tonal relationship, made the bright blue, the lush green of summer seem crude and far away. . . . Contact with the winter scene, when the underlying structure of the whole landscape stood out*

so clearly, affected the whole direction of my future work. It left me with the obvious but basic conviction that wherever art ends it begins with nature. (From Newark Museum, 35th anniversary exhibition catalogue, 1944.)

The term realist as it is applied to contemporary painting has acquired a number of contradictory associations. These should be made clear if the aims of present-day artists are to be understood. . . . The deeper meanings of nature can only be captured in painting through disciplined form and design. The visual recognizability is actually irrelevant. (From Cincinnati Modern Art Society, *A New Realism* exhibition catalogue, 1941.)

See: Forbes Watson, A Note on Niles Spencer, *The Arts*, Sept. 1925, pp. 166–169. M. Mannes, Niles Spencer, Painter of Simplicities, *Creative Art*, July 1930, pp. 58–61. E. W. Watson, Interview with Niles Spencer, *American Artist*, Oct. 1944, pp. 14–17. Holger Cahill, Niles Spencer, *Magazine of Art*, Nov. 1952, pp. 313–15. Henry McBride, Niles Spencer, Elegant American Painter, *Art News*, Mar. 1954, pp. 20–21.

SPENCER:

Erie Underpass,
1949.

Oil, 28 x 36.
Metropolitan
Museum of Art.

GEORGIA O'KEEFFE

by James Thrall Soby

IN 1916 a group of sketches by Georgia O'Keeffe was taken to Alfred Stieglitz by a mutual friend, and her distinguished career as a painter began. O'Keeffe's training as an artist had been received from such divergent teachers as William Chase and Arthur Dow. But she was self-taught in the sense of having developed alone, during a long period of introspection and experiment, the burnished lyricism of vision and technique by which she is now widely known. Born in Sun Prairie, Wisconsin, in 1887, O'Keeffe's human personality is exceptionally integral with her art: severe in its beauty; warm, direct and unafraid.

The subjects of O'Keeffe's painting were decided upon early and have been explored and re-explored—flowers and the city, mountains, bones and simplified elements of architecture, among others. Her art under-

O'KEEFFE: *Black Abstraction,* 1927.

Oil, 30 x 40. Metropolitan Museum of Art, Alfred Stieglitz Collection.

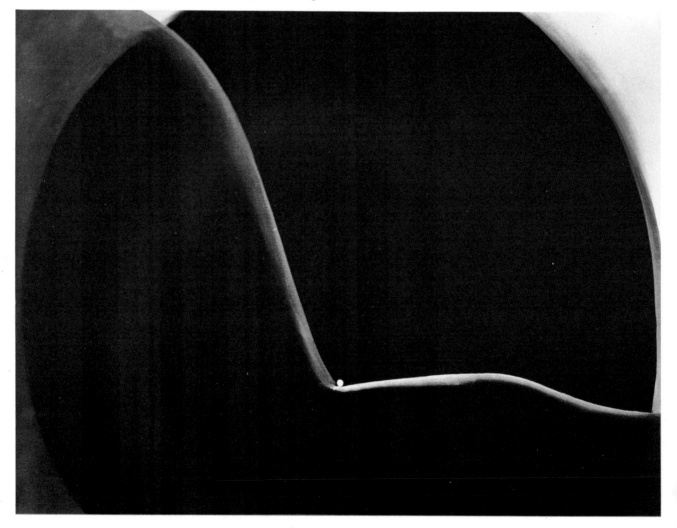

O'KEEFFE: *Black Iris*, 1926. Oil, 36 x 30. Metropolitan Museum of Art, Alfred Stieglitz Collection.

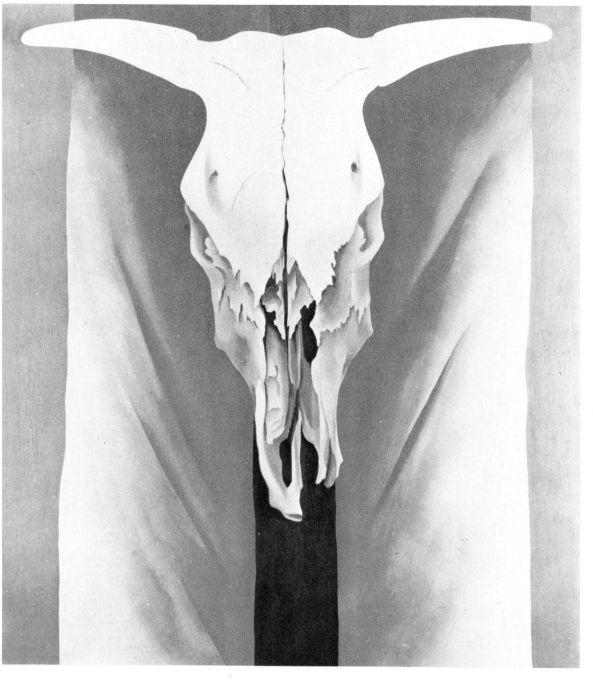

goes an intense process of conceptual purification; she strives relentlessly to discover in plastic terms the essence of a given inspiration. "I found," she wrote in 1923, "that I could say things with color and shapes that I couldn't say in any other way—things that I had no words for."

She loves the landscape and dry light of New Mexico and now lives there most of the time. Recently, however, she visited Spain and was apparently more impressed by the bull fights than by the Prado. There is something appropriate in this fact, for O'Keeffe has been nourished by dramatic tensions within tangible reality more often than by the art of the past or the present. (Among modern painters she especially admired the late Arthur Dove but remains uninfluenced by his work.) Whether her absorption in bullfighting's ritual will one day result in specific pictures, no one yet can say. But surely it will have its effect on that profound and solitary emotional awareness of which the distillate is her art. "The art of Georgia O'Keeffe," Daniel Catton Rich wrote in the catalogue of her 1943 retrospective exhibition at the Art Institute of Chicago, "is a record of intense emotional states resolved into crystalline forms. Her ability to charge abstract elements of line, color, and mass with passionate meanings is as notable as her fastidious and immaculate craftsmanship."

See: Art Institute of Chicago, *Georgia O'Keeffe* exhibition catalogue by Daniel Catton Rich, 1943.

O'KEEFFE:

Lake George Window,
1929.

Oil, 40 x 30. Museum of Modern
Art, Richard D. Brixey Bequest.

O'KEEFFE:

White Canadian Barn,
No. 2, 1932.

Oil, 12 x 30. Metropolitan
Museum of Art, Alfred Stieglitz
Collection.

PHILIP EVERGOOD

by John I. H. Baur

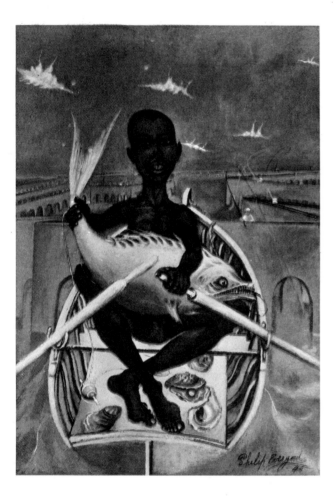

EVERGOOD: *Dream Catch,* 1946.

Oil, 30 x 24. Joseph H. Hirshhorn.

PHILIP EVERGOOD was born in an artist's studio (his father's) in New York in 1901. His mother was English, and from the age of eight he was educated in a variety of English schools, entering Cambridge in 1919. On a trip to Brussels earlier that year, he had become interested in the old masters and had begun to think of studying art. In 1921 he decided to become a sculptor and left the university to work in London with Havard Thomas and with Henry Tonks at the Slade School. Returning to the Art Students League in New York in 1923, he concentrated on drawing although George Luks tried to persuade him to paint.

Evergood was in Paris in 1924, working briefly at the Academie Julian, then for a year in his own studio where he first started to use oil, doing still lifes and an occasional model. Wandering through Italy and southern France, he continued his studies independently. At twenty-five he returned to America where he completed a series of imaginative biblical subjects which won him his first one-man exhibition at the Dudensing Gallery in 1927. Two years later he made his last trip abroad, working chiefly in France and for six months (1930–31) in Spain, where he was deeply impressed by El Greco. Back in New York in 1931, he married Julia Cross and settled in America for good.

The hardship of the depression years affected Evergood profoundly. Like many other painters, he became deeply concerned with problems of social justice, forming strong sympathies and convictions which have never left him. About 1932 he abandoned his biblical themes and began to paint subjects drawn from his own experience and from the life of the working man. Throughout his mature years he has championed many allied causes, taking an active part in the Artists Union, the American Artists Congress and various movements aimed against racial discrimination, fascism and the exploitation of labor. All of his three large murals deal, wholly or in part, with farm and factory work.

But from the beginning Evergood has been different from most social-protest artists, both in attitude and style. Much of his work is not protest at all but an affirmation of human values or, occasionally, pure fantasy. As a painter he mixes the expressive distortions of child art with those of sophisticated mannerists like El Greco, and will suddenly contrast these with passages of extreme realism and rich surface. Alternating between tenderly restrained images and the most theatrical heroics, working one minute in a vein of bitter satire, the next in one of humorous exaggeration, Evergood has emerged as one of our most varied and

PHILIP EVERGOOD   113

EVERGOOD:

Railroad Men, c. 1935.

Oil. Public Works of Art Project, size and present location unknown.

unpredictable artists. Yet there are certain threads that run consistently through his work. One of these is his boisterous delight in human variety, whether it be pathetic or heroic, deeply sensual (as in his nudes) or astringent (as in his satires). His lumpy or emaciated or swelling figures all burst the bounds of normal anatomy by their sheer vitality. Even his villains are intensely alive.

The other typical strain in Evergood's work springs from a fantastic beam in his eye that enjoys dreams, miracles and odd symbols and that gives nearly all his work a wild, strange hue. This quality is not surrealism but rather a kind of violence of the imagination which sees everything larger than life and responds with a special intensity of feeling. There is neither doubt nor compromise in Evergood's work. When he fails he fails resoundingly. More often his art is courageous, imaginative and full of humanity as he understands it.

EVERGOOD: *My Forebears Were Pioneers,* 1940.

Oil, 50 x 30. Mrs. Benjamin C. Betner.

114   PHILIP EVERGOOD

Evergood: *My painting reflects what I see and have experienced here—an imperfect mirror whose objective is a world full of mystery, movement and excitement.*

I value structure, honesty, humor, love for my fellow man above all else.

I want my pictures to affect people on the inside— perhaps to disturb, excite, entertain by a little of the poetry I feel in human expression, in the colors, textures, lines and forms.

See: 20 Years Evergood (with introd. by Oliver Larkin), 1946. Elizabeth McCausland, The Plastic Organization of Philip Evergood, *Parnassus,* Mar. 1939, pp. 19–21.

EVERGOOD: *The Jester,* 1950.

Oil, 61 x 78. A.C.A. Gallery.

PHILIP EVERGOOD   115

EVERGOOD: *The New Lazarus*, 1949.

Oil, 48 x 84. Whitney Museum of American Art.

116

BEN SHAHN *by James Thrall Soby*

BORN IN RUSSIA in 1898, the son of a carpenter, Shahn came to this country with his family at the age of eight. His training as a draftsman was early and thorough. Still in his 'teens, he was employed as a lithographer's apprentice and supported himself at this exacting trade during his studies at New York University, City College of New York and the National Academy of Design. His youth as lithographer and student unquestionably accounts in good part for the technical certainty and iconographical richness of his mature work.

It was from the moral pressure of contemporary events, however, that Shahn caught fire as an artist. Returned from two trips to Europe in the late 1920's, he suddenly became aware that art for him could not be reduced to terms of esthetic sensation alone, that humanity's woes and evils were his instinctive concern. He thereupon painted series of small gouache pictures on the celebrated cases of Sacco-Vanzetti and Tom Mooney. Throughout the 1930's and 1940's, Shahn continued to put his talents to public-social use, painting murals for Federal buildings, designing posters whose strength is their compassion, expressed through eloquent pictorial means.

But Shahn has never ceased being one of the most lyrical and individual of our contemporary easel painters, steadily more fluent, unflagging in invention and never forgetful of the human pulse. At times recently his art has become relatively abstract by comparison

SHAHN: *Sound in the Mulberry Trees,* 1948.

Tempera, 48 x 36. Smith College Museum of Art.

SHAHN:

The Passion of Sacco and Vanzetti, 1931–32.

Tempera, 84½ x 48. Whitney Museum of American Art, gift of Mr. and Mrs. Milton Lowenthal in memory of Juliana Force.

SHAHN: *Ave*, 1950.

Tempera, 31 x 52. Wadsworth Atheneum, Hartford.

SHAHN: *Handball,* 1939.

Tempera, 24 x 33¼. Museum of
Modern Art, Mrs. John D. Rockefeller,
Jr., Purchase Fund.

SHAHN:

*Composition with Clarinet and
Tin Horn,* 1951.

Tempera, 48 x 36. Detroit
Institute of Arts.

SHAHN: Epoch, 1950.

Tempera, 31 x 52. Philadelphia Museum of Art.

with earlier works. It has never become aloof or contrived. His poetry as an artist is still in the service of his fellow-men. And poetry it is, of a very high order.

Shahn: *The making of a picture is an experience of intense and protracted awareness. The content and qualities of the experience differ widely; they may be intellectual or emotional or merely operative. There may be great doubt and struggle involved in the effort to bring the whole work up to a certain pitch at which it may be arrested and maintained; or the effort may be a flowing, easy one of confident virtuosity, the object still being to arrest and make permanent the unique, immediate experience. If the work is successful; if such sustained awareness is impregnated into the physical materials, the colors and forms, so that it dominates and transcends them, then I believe the work lives permanently, communicating its pitch and intensity and arousing a responsive awareness within those persons who look at it.*

That is only the basic aesthetic act, or experience, and it does not touch upon the relative immensity or triviality of the images into which are transmuted the physical materials of art. It is within the stature and kind of the images created that the fuller meanings of art lie. Its primary fact, however, is the crystallizing of a state of awareness.

See: James Thrall Soby, *Ben Shahn*, 1947. Selden Rodman, *Ben Shahn Portrait of the Artist as an American*, 1951. Ben Shahn, *Paragraphs on Art*, 1952. Thomas B. Hess, Ben Shahn Paints a Picture, *Art News*, May 1949, pp. 20–22 ff.

JACK LEVINE

OPPOSITE:

LEVINE: *The Trial*, 1953/4.

Oil, 72 x 63. Art Institute of Chicago.

by Frederick S. Wight

LEVINE: *The Feast of Pure Reason,* 1937.

Oil, 42 x 48. Museum of Modern Art (WPA Art Program).

JACK LEVINE   125

LEVINE: *Welcome Home,* 1947.

Oil, 40 x 60. Brooklyn Museum.

126   JACK LEVINE

"TO BRING the great tradition up to date," is Levine's undertaking, and with reason, since he is concerned with the living core of humanity and not with the changes which transform the surface—"considerations of modernity fill me with horror." That is to say, he is a moralist. He deals with man's predicament, and he speaks of injustice, of meanness, poverty and evil chance.

Born in South Boston in 1915, Levine grew up with a seamy city spectacle which he has contrasted ever since with the outraged ideals of a first generation American. At an early age he attracted the attention of a painter-teacher who "sustained the childish process of drawing," and taught him to draw without models, which may account for Levine's precocity. More important, Denman Ross, of the Harvard Department of Fine Arts, became his mentor, opened the world of the museum to him, "banished my ignorance," as he says, and offered him the continuity he treasures.

The WPA days gave a socially conscious orientation to Levine's morality. Such a trend leads to expression-ism. Morality sets love and hate to work, and love and hate must have living people in plain sight; and emotional judgment means distortion. But Levine resists the subjectivity of expressionism, wants something more logical, plans and considers, and controls impulse. In the end it is sermons and satires that he paints.

The young Levine was swept by Soutine, and Rouault was also an inspiration. Then he moved to Greco, and finally to Rembrandt. But there is also a playful neo-romantic side under Rubens' spell. Levine draws strength from these talents of the past, and his rejections, which are many, are aimed at the present. Bringing tradition up to date has produced a somber plastic art in the main, with an increasing concern for the power of light on a dim stage. "Within light and shadow I can express some kind of drama that is most like me."

This drama has varying degrees of depth. It can be profound and poignant, sardonic, witty or satirical. His style changes accordingly, for he has eloquence at his disposal and all the facility that wit requires. He

LEVINE: *Gangster Funeral,* 1952.

Oil, 60 x 72. Whitney Museum of American Art.

is at his best administering punishment, and his chief enemy is the callousness of mankind.

The war put Levine in a uniform not too well tailored for his individualistic nature. His experience led to at least one of his most successful and drastic paintings—which he considers "buoyant"—*Welcome Home.*

The war past, Levine moved to New York, then gave himself a year's interval in Rome. It is only metropolitan city life which can provide the drama which he needs: the fleeting ironies, the haunting glimpses, the extremes.

Levine: *The Cubes and planes and alarm clocks created by man to conquer the problems of this life are for me secondary objects of contemplation. . . .*

Dehumanization seems the keynote of every field of modern endeavor. . . .

Perhaps the most apparent thing about artists of the past is their freedom from crisis and dilemma in the sense we find it. (From Jack Levine, *Modern Artists on Artists of the Past,* Museum of Modern Art, April 22, 1952.)

See: Museum of Modern Art, *Americans 1942* exhibition catalogue, ed. by Dorothy C. Miller, 1942, pp. 86–92. Institute of Contemporary Art, Boston, *Jack Levine* exhibition catalogue, 1952, pp. 2–16.

THOMAS HART BENTON

by Lloyd Goodrich

THOMAS HART BENTON, born in 1889 in Neosho, Missouri, comes of a family prominent in state and federal politics. Going to Paris in 1908 for three years and becoming a close friend of Stanton Macdonald-Wright, he attempted in his early work to combine Synchromism and classic composition. But after the first World War he rejected the modernist philosophy, and began painting American history in a style based on Renaissance concepts of design.

During ten years, from 1924, Benton travelled widely through the rural South and Midwest, on foot and by car, observing people and places, and making thousands of drawings. This region was still virgin territory for art, untouched since the nineteenth-century genre painters. Benton's drawings, alive with native character, became the raw material for his paintings from the late 1920's, which form a panorama of the America he loves best—the primitive, backwoods America of mountaineers, dirt farmers, negro cotton pickers, small towns, revival meetings, moonshiners, mules and hillbilly musicians. He has a zest for the folk flavor of this America, its crude toughness, its old-fashioned virtues and sins. He pictures it with the sympathy of one who belongs to this soil, and at the same time with that wild flamboyant humor that has come down from the pioneers, from the Mississippi boatmen and Mark Twain. No objective realist, he is an artist with a mission, determined to express his concept of what is most American.

His style is far from literal naturalism. He cares chiefly for the concept of a thing, its animating principle; and he takes liberties with proportions and relations in a way that reminds one of the early Italian primi-

BENTON:

The Sun Treader—Portrait of Carl Ruggles, 1934.

Tempera, 45 x 38. Nelson-Atkins Gallery, Kansas City, Friends of Art Collection.

tives. He has a strong sense of the grotesque, not only in people but in objects and even the face of nature: shacks have as much animation as their inmates, a tractor is an aggressive animal, hills become miniature mountains. This caricatural vein harks back to American graphic humorists from Nast to the comic-strip artists. Everything in his pictures is concrete and tangible, can be touched and grasped; and every form is governed by emphatic rhythmic movement. The keynote of his style is a furious energy, crowding into the picture every possible ounce of plastic existence.

Benton's gifts are especially suited for mural painting, and in a series of ambitious murals executed from 1930 on, he achieved a synthesis of his conception of America—its multiform aspects of work and play, its dynamism and epic proportions. The first to break with the bankrupt pseudo-classicism of academic American mural art, he introduced a vital contemporary viewpoint which has had wide influence.

In the 1930's Benton was the most articulate champion of regionalism. The school is now in total eclipse; but Benton has made an important contribution to American art: he pioneered in discovering aspects of America neglected since the days of Bingham and Blythe, and in picturing them with a new frankness and raciness. He has continued to paint the same kind of subjects in much the same style; his recent large-scale figure pieces are his most fully realized works, impres-

BENTON: *Boomtown,* 1928.

Oil, 45 x 54. Rochester Memorial Art Gallery.

THOMAS HART BENTON

BENTON:

Hailstorm, 1940.

Oil, 33 x 40. Joslyn Art
Museum, Omaha.

sive in their substance and power. Though quite counter to prevailing trends, they have qualities that should outlast the taste of the moment.

Benton: *I've had many aims. Some are esthetic, formative, like those involved in the three-dimensional composition I practise where relations between things are set up on advancing and receding planes of an imaginary deep space. Some are procedural, directed to brilliancy, impact and permanence in the use of colors, mediums, grounds, etc. But my chief aims have been more social, more publicly directed. I believe I have wanted, more than anything else, to make pictures, the imagery of which, would carry unmistakably* American meanings *for Americans and for as many of them as possible.*

See: Thomas H. Benton, American Artists Group, N. Y., 1945.
Thomas Hart Benton, *An Artist in America,* 1951.

BENTON: *Preparing the Bill,* 1934.

Oil, 38 x 46. The artist.

BENTON: *July Hay*, 1943.

Egg tempera and oil, 38 x 26¾. Metropolitan Museum of Art.

132

GRANT WOOD *by James Thrall Soby*

WOOD: *Woman with Plants,* 1929.

Oil, 9½ x 13. Cedar Rapids Art Association.

OF THE ARTISTS who became famous as leaders of the mid-Western regionalist movement of the late 1920's and 1930's, the most estimable surely was Grant Wood of Iowa (1891–1942). Though he spent most of his short life in his native state, Wood seems to have been less vociferously chauvinistic than his confreres in regionalism, perhaps remembering that devotion to a given locale was nothing new or final among artists and had characterized the members of the Hudson River and Barbizon Schools, to mention only two conspicuous examples from the previous century. For all his isolation Wood was a sensitive if homespun esthete, who designed interiors and stained-glass windows and constructed surrealistic objects out of odd materials. The greatest experience of his formative years as an artist was probably his trip to Munich in 1928, when he studied Flemish and German paintings of the fifteenth and sixteenth centuries and came home to apply their immaculate, cautious example to his own work.

At its best this work is of enduring interest because Wood was able to create an American and thoroughly personal imagery from what he had learned abroad. *American Gothic* and *Daughters of Revolution* are well painted pictures. They are also acute in satirical force, a fact alternately conceded and denied by the artist, depending on the degree of hurt or hostile pressure from their living models. We are not likely soon to forget the dour, honest vigor of the figures in *American Gothic* (posed for by Wood's sister and his dentist), nor the acid-mouthed righteousness of his ladies from the D.A.R., nor the wry humor of *Parson Weems' Fable,* with the mature Washington re-enacting his apocryphal childhood. In lesser works than these, however, Wood fell back on repetitious Baroque mannerisms of design, notably in his many Iowan landscapes.

See: Darrell Garwood, *Artist in Iowa, A Life of Grant Wood,* 1944.

OPPOSITE: WOOD: *Parson Weems' Fable,* 1939.

Oil, 46 x 58. Mrs. John P. Marquand.

WOOD: *Daughters of Revolution*, 1932. Oil, 20 x 40. Edward G. Robinson.

WOOD: *Adolescence*, 1940.

Oil, 21 x 13. Abbott Laboratories.

WOOD: *American Gothic*, 1930. Oil, 29⅞ x 25. Art Institute of Chicago, Friends of American Art.

JOHN KANE *by Dorothy C. Miller*

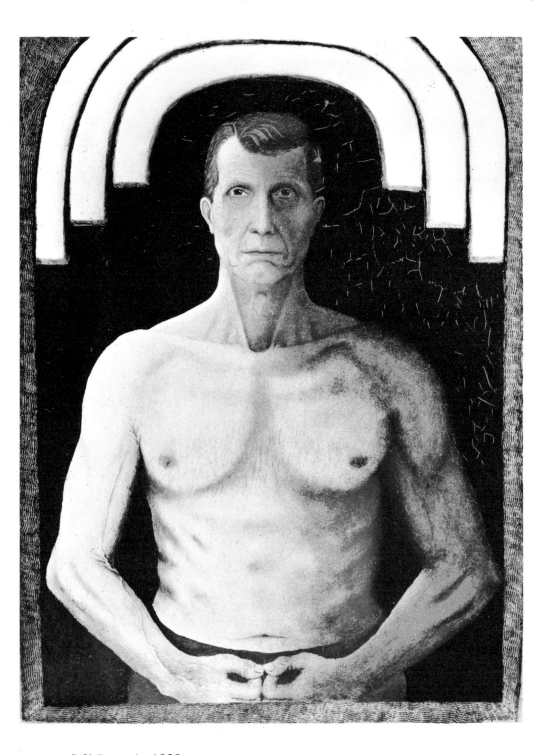

KANE: *Self Portrait*, 1929.

Oil, 36⅛ x 27⅛. Museum of Modern Art, Mrs. John D. Rockefeller, Jr. Purchase Fund.

KANE: *From My Studio Window*, 1932.

Oil, 22¼ x 34½. Extended loan from Miss Adelaide M. de Groot to the Museum of Modern Art.

JOHN KANE (formerly Cain) was a skilled workman at many trades. He was born of Irish parents in 1860 in West Calder near Edinburgh, Scotland. When he was nine he went into the coal mines where he worked until he was nineteen. In 1880 he came to America, settling in Pittsburgh. For years he worked in the coke ovens and blast furnaces, then for years he laid cobblestones in the streets of Pittsburgh. Then he got a job painting freight cars. Through the years he suffered great poverty and traveled about as an itiner-ant laborer in Pennsylvania, West Virginia and Ohio in search of work. About 1909 he became a carpenter and worked building rubber factories in Akron. During the first World War he worked in an ammunition plant and after the war on bridge construction. In the 1920's he was a carpenter and house painter. In 1929, at the beginning of the depression, he painted his last house when almost seventy years old.

It was his experience in painting freight cars which taught Kane the mixing of colors and started him off on

KANE: *Turtle Creek Valley, 1922.*

Oil, 34¼ x 44. Roland P. Murdock Collection, Wichita Art Museum.

KANE:

Scotch Day at Kennywood, 1933.

Oil, 19⅞ x 27⅛.
Museum of Modern
Art, gift of Mr. and
Mrs. Albert Lewin.

his career as a Sunday painter. He tried to get into art classes at the Carnegie Institute and elsewhere but could never afford them. Once, when out of work, he tried to sell portraits, which he made by painting over enlarged photographs, for $3 to $10 each. He even applied for a job assisting John W. Alexander on his Carnegie Institute murals.

When he was about fifty years old Kane got into the habit of carrying sketching materials wherever he went, and began to spend all his spare time drawing and painting. Pittsburgh with its mills, its Scottish festivals, its slum streets, rivers and bridges, its hillsides smoking with industry, gave him the subject matter he loved. It is estimated that he finished about ninety canvases. In 1925 and 1926 he submitted to the jury of the Carnegie International Exhibition but was rejected. In 1927 Andrew Dasburg, a member of the jury, succeeded in getting Kane's painting accepted and bought it himself, and the old workman emerged at last as a recognized artist. The last seven years of his life brought him fame, but he died in poverty of tuberculosis in 1934.

Kane was the folk poet of his adopted city. He painted in direct response to his environment, seeing the hillside and river communities along the Mononga-

hela, the Allegheny and the Ohio with the intense and simple-hearted affection of a child. He had the artisan's respect for his medium, a sure feeling for surface and pattern, and the craftsman's insistence upon exactness and carefully studied detail. "One thing I cannot abide is sloppy work in any form," he said. "I think a painting has a right to be as exact as a joist or a mold or any other part of building construction." Once when asked why he painted he said: "With art comes goodness and beauty."

Kane: *I find beauty everywhere in Pittsburgh. . . . The city is my own, I have worked on all parts of it, in building the blast furnaces and then in the mills and in paving the tracks that brought the first street cars. . . . The filtration plant, the bridges that span the river, all these are my own. Why shouldn't I want to set them down when they are to some extent children of my labors and when I see them always in the light of beauty?* (From *Sky Hooks,* below.)

See: Sky Hooks, The Autobiography of John Kane, as told to Marie McSwigan, 1938. Museum of Modern Art, *Masters of Popular Painting,* exhibition catalogue by Holger Cahill and others, 1938, pp. 118–21. Sidney Janis, *They Taught Themselves,* 1942, pp. 76–98. John O'Connor, Jr., The Kane Memorial Exhibition, *Carnegie Magazine,* April 1936, pp. 19–24.

JOHN KANE   143

EDWARD HOPPER

by Lloyd Goodrich

OPPOSITE:

HOPPER: *Lighthouse at Two Lights,* 1929.
  Oil, 29 x 43. Richard D. Tucker.

HOPPER: *Skylights,* 1926.
  Watercolor, 14 x 20. Mrs. Gregory Stainow.

THE PHYSICAL FACE of America, seen with complete candor, is the material of Edward Hopper's art. But with all his objectivity he is essentially a poet—one who finds his poetry less often in nature than in man's creations, in the structures and cities man has built and among which his life is spent. Hopper's work is an intense expression of that poetry of places which has been a theme of artists through the centuries, from Guardi to Meryon.

Born in 1882 at Nyack, N.Y., studying art in New York, Hopper made three trips to Europe before 1910 which had little effect on his art. As early as 1908 he began painting the American scene in much the same style as today, but it was not until the 1920's that he achieved recognition.

Hopper has discovered for art those man-made features which we now see as most characteristic of the American landscape, but which had been shunned by his more tender-minded predecessors. He likes American architecture in its most frankly native phases, especially the bare white wooden houses and churches of New England. He likes stark, structural things: factories, bridges, the simple immaculate forms of lighthouses. He likes railroads, highways, gasoline stations.

Although human beings appear in his paintings, the whole scene is what interests Hopper. In his city pictures, it is not the hurrying crowds, the traffic and movement, but the city itself—its streets, buildings, its great masses of stone and steel, its varying architecture, its myriad forms. The few human figures are parts of the scene rather than leading actors; often they seem isolated and solitary.

By contrast with impressionism, Hopper's art is built on form. Everything is solidly constructed; the forms are massive and severely simplified; only essentials are given. His paintings are very thoughtfully designed:

HOPPER: *Early Sunday Morning*, 1930.

Oil, 35 x 60. Whitney Museum of American Art.

straight lines are stressed, and strong contrasts of verticals and horizontals create pictorial drama. A frequent device is a straight foreground line, such as a road or railroad tracks, forming a base for the whole. His compositions are monumental rather than dynamic. Always they possess order, balance, and a total harmony.

Unlike the immaculates, an important element in his work is the mood of the scene: the exact time and weather and light, and the emotions which these evoke. Light plays a leading part in his pictures. The American impressionists had imported the soft air and light of France; but Hopper loves the strong sunlight, clear air and high cold skies of the northern United States. He likes the play of sunlight and shadow on white-painted houses; the precise effect of the baking noonday sun on wood, stone, brick; the low light of clear afternoons, modelling the forms of earth and houses. Often his pictures have a crystalline clarity, and give a sense of stillness and waiting, and of loneliness, penetrating and yet serene.

Hopper: *Great art is the outward expression of an inner life in the artist, and this inner life will result in his personal vision of the world. No amount of skillful invention can replace the essential element of imagination. One of the weaknesses of much abstract painting is the attempt to substitute the inventions of the intellect for a pristine imaginative conception.*

The inner life of a human being is a vast and varied realm and does not concern itself alone with stimulating arrangements of color, form, and design.

The term "life" as used in art is something not to be held in contempt, for it implies all of existence, and the province of art is to react to it and not to shun it.

Painting will have to deal more fully and less obliquely with life and nature's phenomena before it can again become great. (*Reality,* Spring 1953, p. 8).

See: Museum of Modern Art, *Edward Hopper Retrospective Exhibition* catalogue, 1933. Lloyd Goodrich, *Edward Hopper,* The Penguin Modern Painters, 1950.

HOPPER:

Cape Cod Evening,
1939.

Oil, 30 x 40. John Hay
Whitney.

HOPPER:

Gas, 1940.

Oil, 26¼ x 40¼.
Museum of Modern
Art, Mrs. Simon
Guggenheim Fund.

EDWARD HOPPER 147

148

CHARLES BURCHFIELD

by Lloyd Goodrich

AS HOPPER is a portraitist of the East, Charles Burchfield is an interpreter of that section of the Middle West where he has lived all his life. Born in Ashtabula, Ohio, in 1893, he spent his youth in Salem, Ohio, and studied at the Cleveland Museum School of Art. Since 1921 his home has been Buffalo, N. Y., and the nearby suburb of Gardenville. His subjects have been drawn almost entirely from this region—a rolling countryside of great distances and wide skies, dotted with small towns and grim industrial cities.

Burchfield began as a romantic. In his early twenties, 1916 to 1918, he painted a series of remarkable imaginative watercolors expressing a highly personal nature poetry. Based partly on childhood memories, they recreated a child's delights and fears. They gave a soul to inanimate things, showing houses like human beings, storm-clouds like monsters; they even visualized sensations of sound and heat. Their style was free and bold in its linear rhythms and strong decorative patterns. At this time Burchfield had seen no modern European art, and his expressionism was an original invention.

This phase lasted only a few years. From subjectivism Burchfield turned to realistic portrayal of the world around him — dreary streets of unpainted wooden houses with false fronts, monstrous mansions of the Garfield era, gray rows of identical workers' homes—the Mid-West country and what man has made of it. But beneath his realism was still the romantic, now in revolt against the ugliness of his environment. His satire was mingled with a compelling expression of mood and a dramatic sense that often approached tragedy. And

BURCHFIELD:

Church Bells Ringing—Rainy Winter Night, 1917.

Watercolor, 30 x 19. Cleveland Museum of Art, the Henry G. Keller Memorial.

BURCHFIELD: *The Night Wind*, 1918.

Watercolor, 21¼ x 21¾. A. Conger Goodyear.

BELOW:

BURCHFIELD: *Promenade*, 1927–28.

Watercolor, 32 x 42. A. Conger Goodyear.

152

BURCHFIELD: *Six O'Clock,* 1936.

Watercolor, 24 x 30. Syracuse Museum of Fine Arts.

always he remained aware of nature; even in the drab towns he was alive to the season, the weather, the time of day. He saw a melancholy poetry in wintry cities with soft-coal smoke and dirty snow—a stir of joy in February thaws, with puddles in the mean streets heralding the approach of spring. His style, with all its realistic power, was essentially baroque, full of movement, delighting in the ornate and complex. Using watercolor almost entirely, he achieved a scale and completeness equal to oil, enormously increasing the range of the medium.

In 1943 began a third phase in Burchfield's development: an abrupt return to the fantasy of his early work, but now on a much larger scale. Again his dominant theme has become the life in nature—the cycle of the seasons, the drama of death and renewal, the miracle of growth, the moving pageant of weather, light and hour. Pervaded by a mystical pantheism, his art has become an ecstatic praise of God in nature. Movement fills the whole picture: wind blows, rain pelts, snow swirls, light breaks through clouds. This sense of life expands into all nature's myriad forms,

down to the smallest—leaf and flower, bird and insect. In these recent compositions, the imaginative poetry which first appeared in his youth now expresses itself with the mature power of realization developed in his middle period. In their wealth of imagery, their dynamism, their baroque profusion, they are among the most remarkable products of the romantic imagination in our time.

Burchfield: *To pursue beauty self-consciously seems to me to miss the whole point in expressing life; beauty, if it happens, must be a by-product, not an aim. Nothing in the world is commonplace. An artist should have an innocent eye, to which nothing is either beautiful or ugly but full of interest and worthy of recording.*

Much has been said about an artist expressing the age he lives in. To me this is the ultimate fallacy. An artist must be a leader who will show his fellow-men a more noble world, which, if it never exists anywhere but in the mind, is the only one worth pursuing.

See: Albright Art Gallery, *Charles Burchfield* exhibition catalogue, 1944. John I. H. Baur, *Charles Burchfield,* 1956.

154   CHARLES BURCHFIELD

BURCHFIELD: *The Coming of Spring,* 1917–43.

Watercolor, 34 x 48. Metropolitan Museum of Art.

KUNIYOSHI:

Little Joe with Cow, 1923.

Oil, 28 x 42. Mrs. Edith Gregor Halpert.

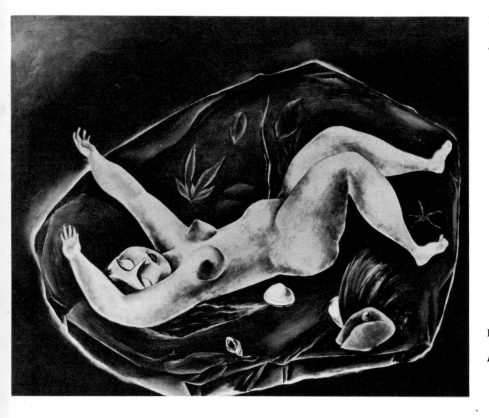

KUNIYOSHI:

Island of Happiness, 1924.

Oil, 24 x 30. Collection William H. Lane Foundation.

YASUO KUNIYOSHI

by Lloyd Goodrich

YASUO KUNIYOSHI was born in Okayama, Japan, about 1890. Coming to the United States in 1906, without friends or money, he went through years of hardship, studying art when he could, and finding his most enlightened teacher in Kenneth Hayes Miller at the Art Students League. His early paintings and drawings, from 1920 on, were the work of a naive, instinctive artist of extraordinary gifts. A unique blend of the Oriental mind and Western technique, they were basically Japanese in their fantasy, their humor, and their interest in all forms of life, down to the most minute—birds and snakes, flowers and weeds, human beings and animals (especially the cow, since he was born in the Year of the Cow). And they were Oriental in their exquisite draftsmanship and their freedom from Occidental ideas of naturalism or perspective. In these early works Kuniyoshi made a highly original contribution to modern art.

Two long visits to France, in 1925 and 1928, produced a more sophisticated viewpoint, closer to contemporary Parisian modernism, and a great gain in skill. Kuniyoshi was a born painter: to him painting was a deeply sensuous process, yielding pure physical pleasure. He loved the pigment itself and its manipulation; he loved textures, ranging from thick impastos to delicate translucent glazes; he loved earthy, resonant color. His brushwork with its sensitive calligraphy was a language in itself. There were no flat or dull passages in his pictures; the whole surface was alive. In his work a rich sensual vitality expressed itself with instinctive artistry.

In middle years his range of subjects was not wide—chiefly women and still-life. His girls in dishabille with

KUNIYOSHI: *Somebody Tore My Poster,* 1943.

Oil, 46 x 26. William Benton.

YASUO KUNIYOSHI   157

their voluptuous impassive faces and their languid pensiveness were embodiments of sexual magnetism. His still-lifes, witty assemblages of seemingly incongruous objects—a vase, a handful of cigars, a pair of binoculars, a toy tiger—not only embodied his zest for forms and colors, but suggested associations beyond the things themselves. This symbolic element in his art increased with the years. Simple naturalism gave way to a growing imaginative character. From 1940 on, his work showed broader human sympathies, a widening social sense, and a new awareness of the state of the world. It was rich in imagery bordering on surrealism, but of a highly individual kind. Its symbolism was never obvious, and often left a final impression of mystery and ambiguity, like much imaginative art. Women still played a central role; they and clowns, masqueraders and circus performers recalled the pleasure principle which had ruled his earlier work—but now they were pictured amid ruins, or in landscapes of poignant desolation. In their mingling of sensualism and melancholy, these paintings seemed to say that the carnival was over. In the work of his last five years, from 1948 until his death in 1953, this ominous dreamlike quality reached an almost hectic intensity. His color flowered into an extraordinary brilliance, with startling new hues—vermilion, saffron, lilac—pushed to extremes of high pitch and planned dissonance. These last paintings, with their gaiety and bitterness, their audacity and sumptuousness, were his most triumphant imaginative achievements. His art had come full circle—from fantasy through naturalism back to fantasy.

Kuniyoshi: *Throughout these many years of painting I have practised starting my work from reality stating the facts before me. Then I paint without the object for a certain length of time, combining reality and imagination. . . . When I have condensed and simplified sufficiently I know then that I have something more than reality.* (From Yasuo Kuniyoshi, East to West, below.)

See: Yasuo Kuniyoshi, East to West, *Magazine of Art,* Feb. 1940, pp. 72–83. Lloyd Goodrich, *Yasuo Kuniyoshi,* 1948.

KUNIYOSHI: *Headless Horse Who Wants to Jump,* 1945.

Oil, 57 x 35. Museum of Cranbrook Academy of Art.

KUNIYOSHI:

Amazing Juggler, 1952.

Oil, 65 x 40. Des Moines Art Center.

YASUO KUNIYOSHI, 159

160

GEORGE GROSZ

by John I. H. Baur

GROSZ: *Couple,* 1934.

Watercolor, 25¼ x 17¾. Whitney Museum of American Art.

WHEN GEORGE GROSZ stepped off the boat in New York on a hot spring day in 1932, he was already a famous German caricaturist. He had been born at Stolp in 1893, trained in the rigorous academies of Dresden and Berlin, and had just reached maturity at the time of the first World War. Hating the army, in which he served twice, bitterly disillusioned by the moral decay of post-war Berlin, Grosz had been drawn, almost against his will, into the biting social satire which won him an international reputation and eventually the active disapproval of the Nazis.

His reaction to America was totally unexpected. He felt as if an oppressive weight had been lifted from his spirits, as if he had escaped into a miraculously sane and normal world. To the disappointment of many critics who were waiting to see what his acid pen would do with American foibles, he gave up caricature and turned, instead, to watercolors of the city, soon followed by landscapes, baroque still lifes and creamy nudes painted in flowing, Rubensesque lines. Outwardly he has lived the uneventful life of a Long Island suburbanite, first at Bayside until 1936, for the next ten years at Douglaston, since then at Huntington. In 1938 he became an American citizen.

But from the beginning there was, as Grosz puts it, "a certain horror in me"—a dark foreboding of disaster which was realized when the second World War finally overwhelmed Europe. Unbidden, his mind and then his brush began to dwell on the senseless destruction, the brutality, the mass murder invoked by the dictators. The pictures that resulted were powerful

OPPOSITE:

GROSZ: *The Pit,* 1946.

Oil, 60¼ x 37¼. Roland P. Murdock Collection, Wichita Art Museum.

GROSZ: *A Piece of My World, I*, c. 1938.

Oil, 32 x 24. Newark Museum.

164

GROSZ: *Waving the Flag*, 1947–48.

Watercolor, 25 x 18. Whitney Museum of American Art.

there is nothing else to do. More often his pictures were purely symbolic. *The Pit* unites, in one swirling, baroque pattern, figures which are vivid embodiments of hunger, madness, prostitution, drunkenness, political chicanery, death and a bloody Europe. It is a kind of modern world apocalypse. In still another vein, Grosz created a legendary gray world peopled by his fanatical "stickmen"—a half-insect, predatory tribe that attacks everything human and waves its flag defiantly at the rest of mankind. These paintings are very different from the early Grosz caricatures and even more so from the nudes and landscapes which he was doing at the same time. In their own Gothic, terror-haunted way they are perhaps the most powerful anti-war pictures of our times.

Grosz: *"Take your brush and start in." This maxim, attributed to old Rembrandt, isn't always easy to adhere to, especially in 1953. One could, perhaps, define this as an ice or metal age of art—an age in which an international freezing or metallizing process has appeared. Somewhere along the way the center was lost and the human element left behind.*

Demons, horrors, storms of wrath (hate), naked violence, humiliation, and complete senselessness left their marks on my outlook. I tried to sublimate these impressions into many hundreds of drawings, watercolors, and later, paintings. I admired Strindberg and often felt that his "Inferno" had become a reality. And when the sulphuric fumes cleared away my thoughts returned to nature. I like to work with nature; when I do, I become balanced and peaceful. I had great pleasure in recognition, which is why I like to paint recognizable objects.

See: George Grosz, *A Little Yes and a Big No*, 1946. John I. H. Baur, *George Grosz*, 1954.

symbols of the artist's despair for humanity. Sometimes they grew out of personal associations. *The Survivor* was suggested by thoughts of Grosz's brother-in-law, who was in the German army despite his age, though the concept changed as he worked, into that of a still older man who fights on alone and senselessly because

FRANKLIN C. WATKINS

by John I. H. Baur

FRANKLIN WATKINS is that rare phenomenon of modern times, a good portrait painter. He is many other things as well—a painter of wry humor, of deeply moving religious subjects (almost as unusual as good portraits today), a fine colorist within the rather chalky range he prefers and an expressionist who uses distortion both boldly and subtly.

Watkins' characteristic style developed slowly. Born in New York in 1894, he studied painting at the Pennsylvania Academy of the Fine Arts, with several interruptions, from 1913 to 1918. For the next five years he worked in a New York advertising agency, finding little time for his own art. There followed a year of study in Europe during which he absorbed influences from modern French painting and from such Renaissance masters of distortion as Tintoretto and El Greco. He was thirty-seven when he first received public recognition in a burst of publicity over the award of a prize to his *Suicide in Costume;* he was forty when he had his first one-man exhibition at the Rehn Gallery in 1934.

Since then he has lived quietly in Philadelphia, work-

WATKINS: *Soliloquy,* 1932.

Oil, 25 x 30. Whitney Museum of American Art.

WATKINS: *The Fire Eater,* 1933–34.

Oil, 60¾ x 39. Philadelphia Museum of Art.

WATKINS: *Thomas Raeburn White,* 1940.

Oil, 34½ x 45. Mr. and Mrs. Thomas Raeburn White.

ing with extraordinary deliberation. His first mature work of the early 'thirties was the most obviously expressionist; contours are in constant, broken motion, anatomy and poses are strongly exaggerated, suggesting violent inner tensions. Yet even here an underlying sobriety rules. The architectural lines of the table in *Soliloquy,* and the great empty space above, imprison the twisting figure in a kind of impersonal calm. The mood of sober thoughtfulness becomes more marked in the fine portraits of the late 'thirties and 'forties. Poses are now chosen to illuminate individual character. Distortions are rigidly disciplined to serve the same purpose; they are subtler, permitting an acceptable likeness, but they are also strong enough to impart the artist's interpretation of his subject. The hewn granite look of Justice Roberts' head with its roughened planes and harsh lighting is an impressive example. Returning in recent years to a less realist style, Watkins has forged his own symbols of Death and Resurrection in two huge murals that create their mood principally through gesture and design. Like all his work, they evolved slowly, traversing many changes, for Watkins is a painter of inmost thoughts who finds no ready-made images in nature but must create them from his own deeply pondered ideas, whether of a man's character or the significance of religious experience.

Watkins: *My work is not strongly prompted by displays to my sight. Often the sound of a few words, freed of their intended meaning; the description of an action, not seeing it; thoughts of the portrait subject, not the look, will form motives that press me. My eye is not an infallible image-maker, though sometimes coherent shape emerges from the recollection of things seen in passing. But while my sources are visually impure, I do try to manage that in my pictures the energy they generate shall come back clean. I find comfort in believing I am not alone with this problem.*

See: Franklin C. Watkins, A Painter Talks to His Students, *Magazine of Art,* Dec. 1941. Andrew C. Ritchie, *Franklin C. Watkins,* 1950.

WATKINS: *Justice Owen J. Roberts,* 1947.

Oil, 50 x 40. Law School, University of Pennsylvania.

WATKINS: *Death*, 1948.

Oil, 108 x 172. Henry P. McIlhenny.

RICO LEBRUN

by James Thrall Soby

LEBRUN: *Migration to Nowhere,* 1941.

Gouache, 30 x 48. The artist.

OPPOSITE:

LEBRUN: *Figure in the Rain,* 1949.

Duco, 48 x 30⅛. Museum of Modern Art, gift of Mrs. Robert Woods Bliss.

BORN IN NAPLES, Italy, in 1900, Rico Lebrun at a very early age developed the absorbing interest in draftsmanship which is an earmark of his mature art. His only professional training was received at the night classes of the Naples Academy of Art. One questions whether he needed any formal training at all. His atavistic instinct for drawing was so strong that very likely his remarkable linear proficiency was the result of a relentness self-instruction which continues to this day.

Lebrun came to America in 1924 and has lived here ever since, becoming one of our foremost artists and also, despite his courageous detachment from prevailing, organized movements, an inspirational teacher. He had served in the Italian Army during World War I. Remembering war's horrors, he completed during the early 1940's some pictures of crippled men fleeing a bombardment, their contorted postures summarizing the extraordinary resilience of human energy in the face of disaster. A sensitive, intelligent humanist, Lebrun has always been most interested in subjects involving anguished and violent challenges to the spirit of the living. Whether painting the bloody struggle between man and beast in the West's slaughter houses, or defining the sad patience of Italy's beggars, he has revived the compassionate dramaturgy of the Baroque masters and their 19th-century successors in Romanticism.

Lebrun inevitably was drawn to the theme of the Crucifixion, and on the theme in recent years has completed a long series of pictures, culminating in an immense triptych. In describing the series, he has declared: "My choice of the theme, Crucifixion, was prompted by the constantly repeated history of man's blindness and inhumanity. My painter's language is founded on the belief of a traditional function of art, that is, to communicate, through dramatic presentation, a legend; a story."

Recently Lebrun has been teaching and working at Mexico's *Instituto Allende.* He writes: "As it happens, I am in the midst of the most impressive and hopeful mess you ever saw, and naturally so involved in it that my past work seems miles away." No finished paintings are yet available. But we may be certain that they will have their own unmistakable temperament, controlled by one of the most acute minds and skilled hands in contemporary American art.

See: Donald Bear, Lebrun Paints a Picture, *Art News,* Dec. 1950, pp. 36–39 ff.

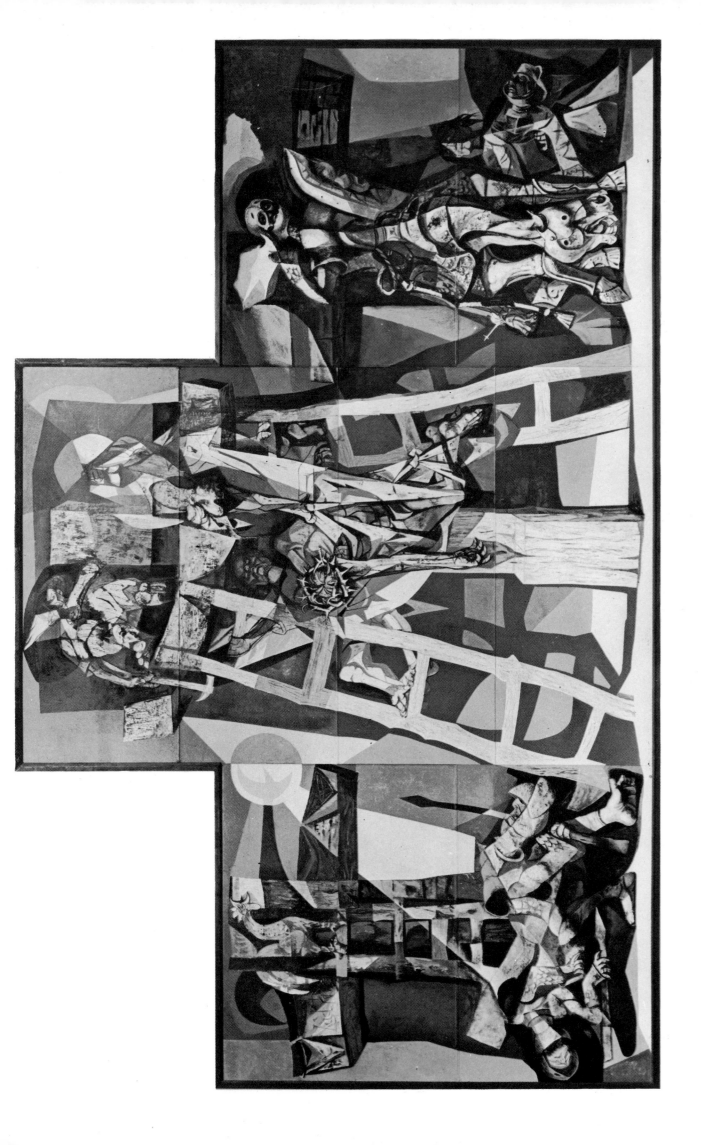

LEBRUN: *Rooster on Arm of The Cross*, 1950.

Duco, 96 x 48. Jacques Seligmann Gallery.

ALFRED MAURER *by Frederick S. Wight*

MAURER: *Le Bal Bullier,* c. 1904.

Oil, 36½ x 38¾. Smith College Museum of Art.

MAURER: *Self-Portrait with Hat,* c. 1927.

Oil, 39 x 23⅞. Walker Art Center, Minneapolis.

TARDY RECOGNITION is all too common, but Alfred Maurer's story is of a birthright missed. One of the earliest converts to the modern movement, he sacrificed to his conversion a success already established, and it was never recaptured.

He was born in New York in 1868, the son of a lithographer for Currier and Ives, Louis Maurer, who put him into the lithographic business at sixteen. Young Maurer gradually drifted toward a painting career, and set sail for Paris at twenty-nine. Here he developed rapidly. Within four years his tasteful Whistlerian style won him a first prize at the Carnegie Institute, and for three more years he repeated this success in exhibitions in America and abroad. But in 1904 he celebrated his birthday by breaking with academic painting, and took his place in the vanguard among the Fauves.

Stieglitz showed him in New York in 1909 along with John Marin, and the next year grouped him with Hartley, Weber and Dove; but Maurer's vivid notations were ill received and he continued to live in France until the first World War forced his return.

Poverty now obliged Maurer to come back into the family home. Louis Maurer, who had been able to retire at fifty, strongly disapproved of his son's newfangled painting, and some inescapable tension developed between him and his son—the aging father on a stepladder watching through a transom as his middle-aged son struggled to paint in his back bedroom on the third floor. Alfred Maurer took an active part in the Independents, and Louis Maurer sent to it too. In 1925 the dealer E. Weyhe made history by buying up all of Maurer's paintings and holding several successful exhibitions, but this was apparently only a palliative and could not cure the morbid thraldom in which Maurer was held.

There was some basic split in Maurer's life, whether the division lay between conservative and modern, between Europe and America, between freedom and a strange psychological captivity. Maurer was a man who had the courage to take a stand but not the strength to win a battle, and his impasse became reflected in his work. About 1919 he began to paint an obsessive series of two girls' heads. These "sisters" are impossibly close, too close for distinct bodies. At times the heads fuse and join, at times recollections of Cubism break them into fragments. They carry a heavy load of self-portraiture and it is hard not to see them as the projected image of the painter's own divided and feminine personality. The transition to the magnificent and accusing *Self-Portrait with Hat* of 1927 is not too great, as though the artist's vision had momentarily cleared, and he had faced himself squarely.

What with the new interest in Americana in the 'thirties, Louis Maurer was given a one man show at the age of ninety-nine—his age was a news item in itself. He lived on through his hundredth birthday, which fell within a day of Washington's two-hundredth anniversary and was sufficient occasion for a further showing of Louis Maurer prints. Alfred Maurer responded to this apotheosis with a portrait of Washington, his last painting as it proved. It is a masterwork of latterday cubism—to allow for the necessary violence—with a black bar across the face of Washington as though it were a cancelled postage stamp.

Louis Maurer died soon after these events in the summer of 1932, and sixteen days later his ailing son hanged himself. Independence was apparently beyond Maurer's strength, but his real independence had gone into his work.

Maurer: *It is necessary for art to differ from nature or we would at once lose the* raison d'être *of painting. Perhaps art should be the intensification of nature; at least it should express an inherent feeling which cannot be obtained from nature except through a process of association. Nature, as we all know, is not consciously composed; and therefore it cannot give us a pure aesthetic emotion.* (From *Forum Exhibition* catalogue, 1916.)

See: Sherwood Anderson, Maurer "Broadside" published by E. Weyhe, Jan. 1924. Walker Art Center and Whitney Museum of American Art, *A. H. Maurer: 1868–1932* exhibition catalogue, ed. by Elizabeth McCausland, 1949. Elizabeth McCausland, *A. H. Maurer,* 1951.

MAURER: *Twin Heads,* c. 1930.

Oil, 26⅜ x 18. Whitney Museum of American Art.

MAURER: *Still Life with Doily*, c. 1930.
Oil, 17¾ x 21½. Phillips Collection, Washington.

STUART DAVIS

by James Thrall Soby

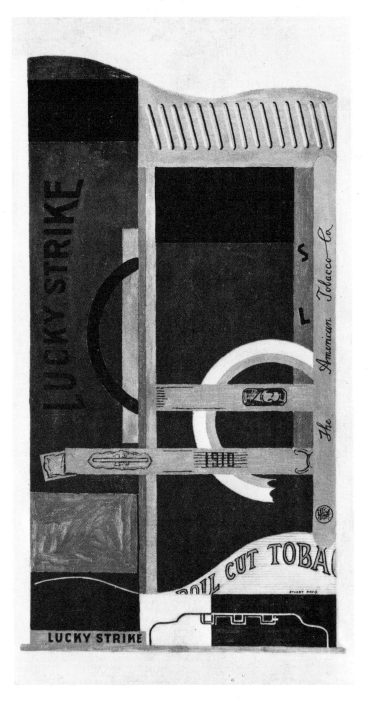

STUART DAVIS' art is, among other things, remarkable for its precociousness and its capacity to renew itself steadily, over a long period of time. Born in Philadelphia in 1894, he was producing altogether personal watercolors and drawings before World War I. He was only nineteen, with several years of training at the Henri School in New York behind him, when the Armory Show startled him into a recognition of the visual revolution that had taken place since impressionism. In 1921 he painted *Lucky Strike,* a picture which holds up well in the toughest European company of cubists and abstractionists in general. Considered as a whole, his early art pays the sort of extra dividend which instinctively creative painters alone can afford.

Davis' mature, steadfast accomplishment over the past thirty years is even more impressive. He returned from two years in Paris (1928–29) more skilled and perceptive than before but at the same time more definitely American in the brash freshness of his vision. The tempo of New York City, the counterbeats of jazz music, the hieroglyphs of public signboards and lettering, the shrieks of thoughtless color in our streets—these have nourished an inner imaginative life which Davis has disciplined rigidly but almost never dulled. He has grown more bold with age, as the strong do; the concentrated abstract solution of *Salt Shaker* leads on to the over-all sweep of *Report from Rockport* and beyond that to the brilliant, spare clarity of *Owh! in San Pao.*

For many years now Davis' position as one of our finest painters in the abstract direction has been secure. Today he seems both more buoyant and convinced than nearly all his younger rivals.

DAVIS: *Lucky Strike,* 1921.

Oil, 33¼ x 18. Museum of Modern Art, gift of the American Tobacco Company.

DAVIS: *Place Pasdeloup*, 1928.

Oil, 36¼ x 28¾. Whitney Museum of American Art.

DAVIS: *Owh! in San Paõ,* 1951.

Oil, 52¼ x 41¾. Whitney Museum of American Art.

184

DAVIS: *Salt Shaker*, 1931.

Oil, 49⅞ x 32. Museum of Modern Art.

Davis: *The essential content of my work is determined by my concept of Purpose. This is derived from an interpretation of the Anatomy of Awareness. I see it as psychological identification with things outside the self, including that physical area of public action called Language. Integral to Awareness is a sense of urgency to choose between the elements that compose it. Choice is made on one's own responsibility, is free, and becomes the physical Shape of Purpose in the Color-Space idiom of painting. Such a Shape in cumulative totality, regardless of the context of ulterior meaning and mood of its individual elements, defines the Reality and Truth of Art.*

See: Stuart Davis, *Stuart Davis,* American Artists Group, 1945. Museum of Modern Art, *Stuart Davis* exhibition catalogue by James Johnson Sweeney, 1945. Frederick S. Wight, Profile of Stuart Davis, *Art Digest,* May 15, 1953, p. 13 ff. Dorothy Gees Seckler, Stuart Davis Paints a Picture, *Art News,* summer 1953, pp. 30–33 ff.

186   STUART DAVIS

DAVIS: *Report from Rockport*, 1940.

Oil, 24 x 30. Mr. and Mrs. Milton Lowenthal.

DAVIS: *Visa*, 1951.

Oil, 40 x 52. Museum of Modern Art, gift of Mrs. Gertrud A. Mellon.

ARSHILE GORKY

by Lloyd Goodrich

ARSHILE GORKY was born in a village on Lake Van in Turkish Armenia, probably in 1904. His native country, wild and mountainous, and the songs and dances of the Armenian people left life-long impressions on his mind and art. During the first World War his family lost everything and his mother died; and in 1920 he came to America. Contending with poverty all his life, he was mostly self-taught. Gorky was an impassioned student of the masters, past and present, haunted the New York galleries and museums, and early became an adherent of advanced art. His evolution showed the successful influences of Cézanne, Picasso, Léger, Chirico, Kandinsky and Miro. But he was far from an uncreative imitator; he learned the language of modern art as a musician learns by composing variations on themes by other composers. His own artistic nature was so deeply sensual, so much in love with pigment and color, that everything he did was himself.

After an early representational phase, as in the retrospective portrait of himself as a child with his mother, he embarked about 1930 on abstract experiments, at first cubistic, then in free non-geometrical forms with a growing surrealist content. By his middle thirties he had assimilated external influences and was expressing himself in terms more and more individual—a development aided by a return to direct contact with nature. Gorky was essentially a lyrical artist, and much of his imagery was based on landscape motifs. Working outdoors in the summer of 1943 he produced scores of colored drawings of leaf and flower forms—studies which contained the germs of his later paintings. Natural objects, already somewhat abstracted in the drawings, were still further abstracted in the paintings—translated into forms existing in their own right but retaining the character of their prototypes in nature. From this time

Gorky's art flowered into a highly personal kind of surrealist abstraction, in which images from nature, memory and the unconscious mind were transformed into visual symbols and embodied in semi-abstract patterns. His style was marked by richly sensuous substance, luxuriant color, and a freedom of touch that was akin to automatic writing. But Gorky was always a draftsman, both precise and powerful, and his seeming improvisation was actually the result of planned design, as proved by numerous studies and successive versions.

In a series of large paintings finished in his last year Gorky attained his greatest plastic inventiveness. In them he expressed fully the passionate poetry of his nature. They are landscapes of the unconscious mind, sometimes conveying sensual delight in earth and heat, sometimes embodying in their imagery the mystery and drama of sex, sometimes pervaded by a brooding sense of tragedy. Their depth of emotion, their richness of symbolism and their maturity of style prove that he was growing year by year. In certain paintings the tragic sense that had always been latent in his work reached a climax of intensity—a climax that presaged his death by suicide when he was only forty-three. A pioneer of the second wave of abstract art, Gorky had a strong influence on the abstract expressionist movement which has dominated the last decade.

Gorky: *The twentieth century—what intensity, what activity, what restless nervous energy! Has there in six centuries been better art than Cubism? No. Centuries will go past—artists of gigantic stature will draw positive elements from Cubism. (Creative Art, Sept. 1931, p. 213.)*

See: Whitney Museum of American Art, *Arshile Gorky Memorial Exhibition* catalogue, text by Ethel Schwabacher, 1951.

GORKY: *The Liver is the Cock's Comb*, 1944. Oil, 73 x 98. Albright Art Gallery.

GORKY: *The Artist and His Mother,* 1926–29.

Oil, 60 x 50. Whitney Museum of American Art, gift of Julien Levy for Maro and Natasha Gorky in memory of their father.

GORKY: *The Betrothal, II,* 1947.

Oil, 50¾ x 38. Whitney Museum of
American Art.

GORKY: *Agony,* 1947.

Oil, 40 x 50½. Museum of Modern Art,
A. Conger Goodyear Fund.

191

MARK TOBEY

by Dorothy C. Miller

MARK TOBEY was born in 1890 in Centerville, Wisconsin, near Trempeleau Bay where, as he says, "from caves in the bluffs one looks down upon the Mississippi a mile wide and islanded in the center. Between the caves and the river are the Indian mounds, rounded forms full of fantastic objects never found. . . ."

As a very young man working in Chicago, Tobey did fashion layouts and admired such illustrators as Christy, Charles Dana Gibson and Fisher. Then he saw the Sorolla exhibition at the Art Institute and discovered Sargent, Zorn, Zuloaga. He studied briefly at the Art Institute but was chiefly self-taught, immersing himself in study of the great artists of the past.

In 1911 Tobey went to New York, where he spent much of the next ten years. His first recognition as an artist came in 1917 when he exhibited a series of portrait drawings in New York. In 1923 he went west, settled in Seattle and taught at the Cornish School. He went to Europe in 1925, lived in Paris, visited the Near East, then returned in 1927 to divide his time between Seattle, Chicago and New York.

From 1931 to 1938 Tobey held the post of artist-in-residence at Dartington Hall in South Devon, England, where he painted a mural. During these years he continued to travel, in Europe, to Mexico, back to Seattle, and finally, in 1934, to Japan and China. In Shanghai he studied with his friend Teng Kwei and learned the rhythm and movement of the Chinese brush, the "pressure and release. Each movement, like tracks in the

TOBEY: *Broadway,* 1936.

Tempera, 26 x 19¼. Metropolitan Museum of Art.

TOBEY: *Above the Earth,* 1953.

Tempera, 40 x 30¼. Art Institute of Chicago, gift of Sigmund Kunstadter.

TOBEY: *Transit,* 1948.

Tempera, 24½ x 18½. Metropolitan Museum of Art.

snow, is recorded and often loved for itself." A series of paintings with bird, snake and moon motifs was done in Shanghai and later shown at the Seattle Art Museum. Back in Seattle in 1935, Tobey painted *Broadway Norm,* a small tempera which pointed the direction of his mature style, employing for the first time the "white writing" which encloses, masks and reveals form in a calligraphic continuity based on the Chinese brush. Lyonel Feininger has called white writing "the handwriting of a painter who . . . has created a new convention of his own, one not yet included in the history of painting." White writing was to prove wonderfully suited to a subject that has moved Tobey greatly—the electric night of American cities.

Tobey worked on the Federal Art Project in Seattle in the late 1930's. Through the 1940's he lived in Seattle, where he had a quiet but profound influence on younger painters. With C. S. Price of Oregon, he has been credited as a founder of modern northwest painting. Tobey held a large retrospective exhibition in 1951 at the California Palace of the Legion of Honor in San Francisco and the Whitney Museum of American Art, New York. In 1954–55 he lived in New York and Paris and held one-man shows in Berne, Paris and London.

Tobey: *Homage—to all the artists I have ever known. To those gone, closer perhaps through a name than the nameless ones, and to those who gave anonymously to the spirit. . . . To the Oriental masters and to the Pacific winds and tides, and the towering Sequoias. . . . To quiet streets and the hum of the great cities. To that which inspired the Red Man's images now looking at me with wide open eyes through glass, gazing beyond to lands not conquered—only the whir of the feathered arrow, then silence surrounding the mystic word now meaningless. Not to be named or numbered, all these, or remembered except as when one gazes eyeless through a window. For what am I but all these—whole at times, or in part, fractioned yet clinging, not sure, as in a game yet playing. No artist ever existed without roots. . . .*

See: Whitney Museum of American Art, *Mark Tobey* exhibition catalogue, 1951. Museum of Modern Art, *Fourteen Americans* exhibition catalogue, ed. by Dorothy C. Miller, 1946, pp. 70–75. Mark Tobey, Reminiscence and Reverie, *Magazine of Art,* Oct. 1951, pp. 228–32. Kenneth Rexroth, Mark Tobey of Seattle, Washington, *Art News,* May 1951, pp. 16–19.

MARK TOBEY 195

TOBEY: *Edge of August,* 1953.
Casein, 48 x 28. Museum of Modern Art.

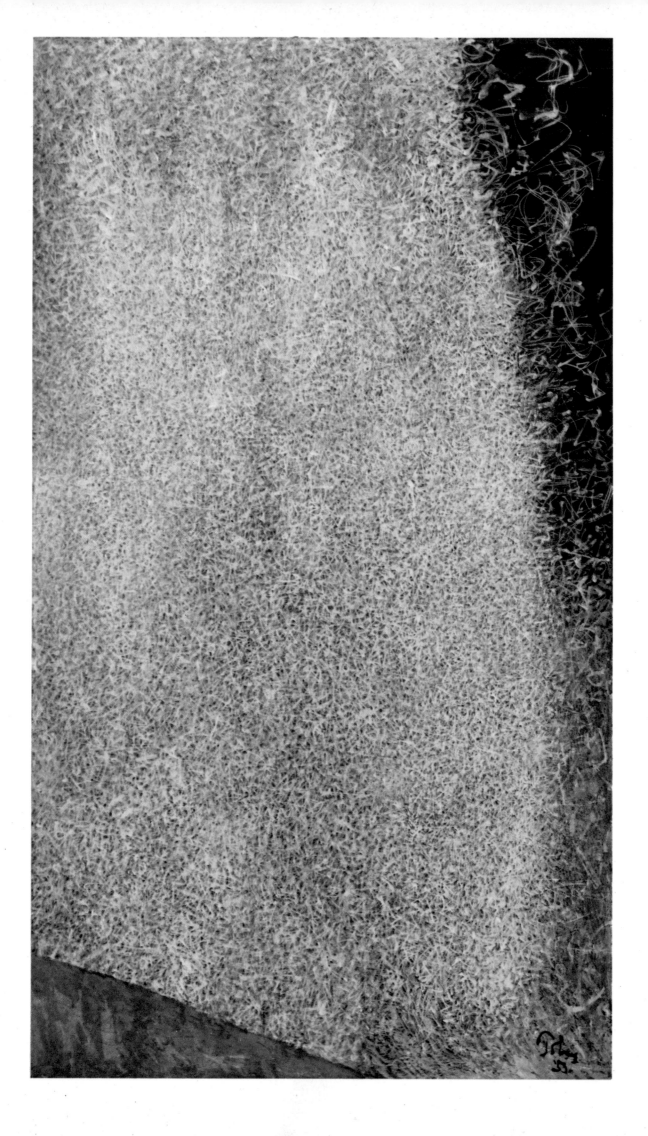

IVAN LE LORRAINE ALBRIGHT

by John I. H. Baur

ALBRIGHT: *Into the World There Came a Soul Called Ida,* 1929–30.

Oil, 56⅛ x 47. Art Institute of Chicago.

IVAN ALBRIGHT is the Thomas Browne of American art—a painter who has dwelt consistently on the corruption of the flesh and the transitory nature of even inanimate things. This might seem strange, for his father, Adam Emory Albright, was a portrayer of American country children, and Ivan (born in Chicago, February 20, 1897) posed with his twin brother Marvin for many idyllic scenes—perhaps too many. His original choice of career was architecture, which he studied at the University of Illinois. He was also painting, and in 1918 he first exhibited publicly in a watercolor show at the Art Institute of Chicago. The same year he joined an American hospital unit in France, where his precise skill as a draughtsman was utilized by the Army to make detailed drawings of wounds and operations, an experience which may have had some bearing on his later work.

In France, Albright decided to become a painter and found time to study briefly at the Ecole des Beaux Arts in Nantes. Returning to America after the war, he continued his studies, first at the Art Institute of Chicago (1919–23), then at the Pennsylvania Academy (1923) finally at the National Academy in New York (1924). In 1925 he settled in Warrenville, Illinois, where he, his father and his brother established themselves in a vacant Methodist church. Later he built a new studio nearby and more recently has divided his time between Chicago and a ranch in Wyoming.

Albright developed the essentials of his mature style soon after leaving school. From the beginning it was an art of strong light and dark contrasts and of a fluid, baroque movement. His figures look as if they had been posed under a single photographic flood light which reveals harshly where it strikes and totally obscures where it shadows. The violent pattern created by these lights and darks flows, in his early work, along massive lines created by the folds of garments and the big forms of a figure. In later pictures, like *Ida,* the design becomes more intricate and the light seems to splinter on the varied textures of wicker, lace and sagging flesh. But virtually all the artist's work, early and late, is conceived in terms of theatrical illumination and restless motion.

As Albright developed, the importance of detail grew and the mood of his pictures darkened. The painterly realism of his first work was gradually transformed into a microscopic realism. Now pores, wrinkles, warts, the individual bristles of an unshaven chin stand out with a clarity that seems grotesque, partly because our vision does not normally probe so closely, partly

ALBRIGHT:

Maker of Images 1928.

Oil, 30 x 20.
William Benton.

ALBRIGHT:

And Man Created God in His Own Image, 1931.

Oil, 48 x 26.
Mrs. Ivan
Le Lorraine Albright.

ALBRIGHT:

Poor Room—There Is No Time, No End, No Today, No Yesterday, No Tomorrow, Only the Forever and Forever and Forever without End, 1942– (unfinished).

Oil, 47 x 37. The artist.

because the very wealth of detail creates a bewildering maze that shocks the eye with cumulative and intimate revelations. Perspective is wrenched in conflicting directions and over these suffering images lie his strange colors—off-blacks and purples that suggest the iridescence of decay.

Albright's penchant for the macabre has twice been utilized by Hollywood—once in 1943–44 when he painted, with his brother, "portraits" of moral dissolution for *The Picture of Dorian Gray,* again in 1945 when he did *The Temptation of Saint Anthony* for *Bel Ami.* Yet the artist's true accomplishment is more profound than the rather theatrical effects of these canvases. The raddled bodies which he creates with such infinite care (one picture took ten years to finish) cage an invincibly human spirit that speaks from their eyes and even from their weary figures. His theme is the tragedy of mortality; his mood acceptance, but not defeat.

Albright: *A picture is like a house wherein all things are to be found, both material and immaterial; it is a place wherein, side by side, rest decay and the sublime; and children's laughter brushes the inner prayer.*

A painting is life and a painting is death, both making and lying in the coffin built for tomorrow's use.

A picture is life, and its life will be no stronger than the days, than the minutes which contain man's desires, frustrations, passions and contemplations; this existence that throws at will, in its mind, chairs or trees, rugs and books, death and meat; a porridge-pot of nights, nightmares and stars. All these and more must go into the picture one does make. This picture will possess no more love than you possess; show no more bewilderment than you betray; be no more sincere than you are; create no more awe than is felt by you.

In essence a painting is an astigmatized portrayal of you; it is your Rorschach with id and plaster cast. It can be no better than you are.

It is essential that we give of the whole and not of the part, for the picture is our legacy left by tomorrow's dead for tomorrow's living.

See: Daniel Catton Rich, Ivan Le Lorraine Albright, *Magazine of Art,* Feb. 1943, pp. 48–51. *Current Biography,* 1944.

ALBRIGHT:

That Which I Should Have Done I Did Not Do, 1931–41.

Oil, 97 x 36. Mrs. Ivan Le Lorraine Albright.

PETER BLUME

by James Thrall Soby

IN CONTEMPORARY American art, Peter Blume
occupies a solitary place. Born in 1906, he has been
painting professionally since 1925 and in that long
time has produced less than seventy pictures in oil.
The greater part of his energy, thought and talent has
been spent creating a few major works—namely
Parade (1930), *South of Scranton* (1931), *Light of
the World* (1932), *The Eternal City* (1934–37) and
The Rock (1945–48). No other living American
painter has been quite so indifferent to time in achieving climactic images: the last two pictures named each
took three years of unflagging concentration to complete. Yet a paradox of Blume's career is that, however
deliberate and painstaking his program, he is constantly
alert to chimerical suggestions, as much interested in
fugitive impressions as in obsessive themes. This fact
partly accounts for his art's vividness and power, quite
apart from its unquestioned technical precision.

Blume came to this country from his native Russia
when he was five. At fifteen he was attending classes
in draftsmanship at the Educational Alliance and later
studied at the Art Students League and the Beaux Arts
Institute of Design. Not yet twenty, he was befriended
by Charles Daniel and at the latter's gallery learned
that his longing for crystalline lucidity in painting was
shared by some of his elders, notably Charles Sheeler,
Charles Demuth and Preston Dickinson. In youth
Blume was fascinated by the clean, hard contours of
machinery and industrial forms. But a strong and

BLUME: *Maine Coast,* 1926.

Oil, 30 x 40. Sturgis Ingersoll.

BLUME: *Light of the World*, 1932.

Oil, 18 x 20. Whitney Museum of American Art.

BLUME: *Parade*, 1930.

Oil, 49¼ x 56⅜. Museum of Modern Art,
gift of Mrs. John D. Rockefeller, Jr.

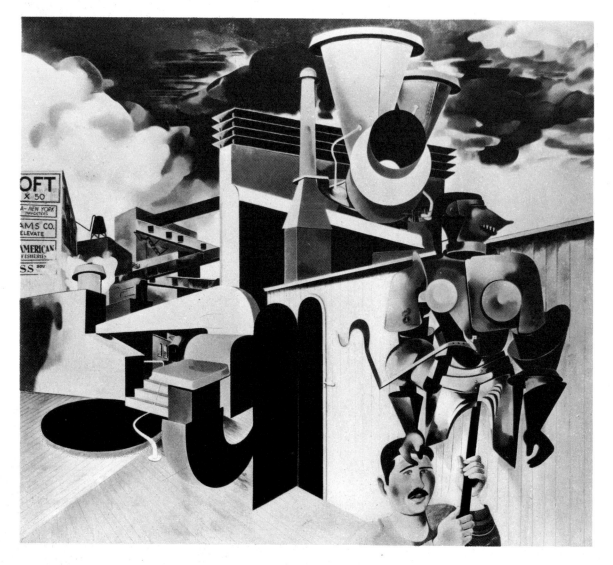

private sense of fantasy was almost always felt in his work, as when in *South of Scranton* German sailors from the cruiser "Emden" (which Blume had seen anchored at Charleston) soar unbelievably high while performing their calisthenic exercises, or when in *Light of the World* figures stare weirdly at a marine light such as Blume had seen at Provincetown and thought of as a "blossom of the sea."

In 1932 Blume went to Italy as a Guggenheim Fellow and there was impressed by the vast array of art and archeological treasures and by the ubiquitous image of Il Duce. The result was *The Eternal City,* a masterwork of 20th-century American painting. Several years later Blume developed an animistic conception of nature and its relationship to man which reached

its climax in *The Rock,* a picture wherein the masonry for Frank Lloyd Wright's superb Kaufmann house at Bear Run is wrested from the surrounding ground. Recently the painter has traveled widely in the Mediterranean and the Orient and probably long since begun that imaginative accrual of visual episodes, both seen and subconsciously felt, which will one day comprise another important work of art.

See: James Thrall Soby, *Contemporary American Painters,* 1948, pp. 51–54.

BLUME: *South of Scranton,* 1931.

Oil, 56 x 66. Metropolitan Museum of Art.

PETER BLUME 207

ALTON PICKENS

by Dorothy C. Miller

ALTON PICKENS was born in Seattle, Washington in 1917. His adolescence was spent under the shadow of the great depression, the rise of Hitler, the Spanish Civil War, Munich. With his schoolmates he watched ships being loaded with scrap-iron for Japan and debated the threat of Japanese or Bolshevik invasion of our West Coast.

At Reed College in Portland, Oregon, which he attended, there were no art courses, but his interest in art was given strong encouragement by Lloyd Reynolds, his professor of English. Pickens went on a scholarship to the Portland Art Museum School but after a few months he was drawn to New York where, he says, he learned from observing artists at work and frequenting the museums. Earning a livelihood at odd jobs, he confined himself for some time to ink drawing and woodcut, slowly learning the oil medium through study of the old masters who, he felt, had the most to teach him. He also greatly admires Goya, Daumier, Bonnard and Beckmann.

Pickens has painted some of the most bizarre, disturbing and memorable images in recent American art. He first exhibited in 1942 at the Metropolitan Museum of Art with a woodcut in *Artists for Victory*. The Museum of Modern Art showed a painting in 1943 and included a group of his paintings in *Fourteen Americans, 1946*; he held his first one-man show in 1956. He has taught art since 1947 at Indiana University in Bloomington, spending a year in Europe in 1952–53.

Pickens: *Perhaps it is sacrilegious to ask why one paints, but if it is an error, it is understandable today. . . .*

My painting concerns itself with man and the traumata of his life. How he constructs and lives by an unending chain of fables, each with its own completeness and each unrelated. . . . I cannot paint reality for what it pretends to be or for what I think it should be.

PICKENS: *Acrobat*, 1947.
Oil, 50 x 34. Mr. and Mrs. Earle Ludgin.

PICKENS: *The Blue Doll,* 1942.

Oil, 42⅞ x 35. Museum of Modern Art, James Thrall Soby Fund.

PICKENS: *Henry Hope Family,* 1950–54.

Oil, 52 x 60. Mr. and Mrs. Henry R. Hope.

I attempt to capture the warping of the truth and the fiction into one schismatic reality. The limitations of my skill and perception compel me to select the minutest aspect of this phantasmagoria, often constituting only a strange ritual of manners, real but senseless. Underlying all is the consciousness that each new hour verifies another intangible—the feeling of imminence and threat that follows the life of any sentient man. (From Alton Pickens, There Are No Artists in Hiroshima, see below.)

See: Museum of Modern Art, *Fourteen Americans* exhibition catalogue ed. by Dorothy C. Miller, 1946, pp. 49–53. Alton Pickens, There Are No Artists in Hiroshima, *Magazine of Art,* Oct. 1947, pp. 236–38.

ALTON PICKENS   211

PICKENS: *Carnival, 1949.*

Oil, 54⅝ x 40⅜. Museum of Modern Art, gift of Lincoln Kirstein.

EDWIN DICKINSON

by Dorothy C. Miller

DICKINSON:

Woodland Scene,
1933–35.

Oil, 71⅜ x 68½.
Andrew D. White
Museum of Art,
Cornell University,
gift of Mrs. Ansley W.
Sawyer.

OPPOSITE:

DICKINSON: *Composition with Still Life,* 1933–37.

Oil, 97 x 77¾. Museum of Modern Art, gift of Mr. and Mrs. Ansley W. Sawyer.

EDWARD DICKINSON 215

DICKINSON: *Self Portrait,* 1941.

Oil, 20 x 23. Mr. and Mrs. Earle Ludgin.

EDWIN DICKINSON was born at Seneca Falls, New York, in 1891. He went to New York City in 1910 to study at Pratt Institute. The following year he studied with Chase at the Art Students League, and then went to Provincetown, Massachusetts, where he worked with Charles W. Hawthorne during the summers of 1912–14. He lived in Provincetown until 1917 when his painting was interrupted by two years' service in the U. S. Navy. After the war he painted for a year in Italy, Spain and France, then returned to live in Provincetown. Two winters were spent in Buffalo, New York, teaching, and in 1937–38 he painted again in Europe. Since 1944 he has taught during the winter in New York, returning to his home on Cape Cod each summer. He visited Europe again in 1952.

Dickinson spends long periods of time on a single composition, slowly elaborating its many elements into a final whole that has the mysterious quality of a vision, an atmosphere of suspense and hallucination. He does not care to write about his work. When pressed for explanations, he willingly identifies objects and figures in his pictures, but throws no light upon the essential mystery of their juxtapositions or the meaning of the symbols. At first glance these complex paintings with their recurrent motifs—foreshortened nudes, a blue rose, fiery coals, rocks falling through space—suggest literary associations or a surrealist attitude. But closer study reveals that this is a completely visual world, dense with objects which, though not easy to identify, come out of exact and searching observation. With purely plastic means Dickinson plays with light and shade and perspective as boldly as the artists of the baroque, and this play he has complicated and enriched through discontinuity in the handling of form and color, here holding and defining forms in clear articulation by light and perspective, there arbitrarily tearing them with shadow and impinging objects, or drifting them away from anchored fact through clouds of paint that turn defining edges into mist and illusion.

See: Elaine de Kooning, Edwin Dickinson Paints a Picture, *Art News,* Sept. 1949, pp. 26–28. Elaine de Kooning, Dickinson and Kiesler, *Art News,* Apr. 1952, pp. 20–23, 66–67. Museum of Modern Art, *Fifteen Americans* exhibition catalogue, ed. by Dorothy C. Miller, 1952, pp. 42–44. *Art News,* Mar. 1955, p. 47.

DICKINSON: *Ruin at Daphne,* 1943–53.

Oil, 48 x 60. Metropolitan Museum of Art, Edward Joseph Gallagher, 3rd, Memorial.

EDWARD DICKINSON   217

THE
WIDENING
SEARCH

1940-1955

Glarner

Pereira

de Kooning

Pollock

Baziotes

Motherwell

Tomlin

MacIver

Graves

Bloom

Lawrence

Wyeth

AMERICAN ART has never experienced so sudden and so spontaneous a change as the general swing towards abstract painting that has taken place during the last fifteen years. Why this occurred is hard to say. Perhaps the catastrophe of another world war made social values seem so· meaningless that the artist turned to more purely esthetic forms of expression. Or it may be that, in the natural course of action and reaction, the time was ripe for a new cycle of abstract experiment and that now we were better prepared, both artistically and critically, by our earlier experience. Whatever the causes, abstraction became the dominant trend in our creative painting soon after 1940.

A striking feature of the new movement has been its diversity. Our pioneer abstractionists—men like Weber, Dove and Stuart Davis—brought their highly individual styles to a mature flowering and began to have a considerable influence on younger painters. Other artists reinvestigated virtually all the traditional forms of European abstraction and adapted these to their own needs. Thus we have had revivals of cubism, futurism and an especially vigorous American school of geometrical abstraction, strongly influenced by the Dutch painter Mondrian.

But by far the most fertile and popular form of abstraction grew out of surrealism and, like it, has been deeply introspective in nature. One of the first to develop in this direction was Arshile Gorky, soon joined by a brilliant group of younger painters including Jackson Pollock, Willem de Kooning, Robert Motherwell, William Baziotes and the somewhat older Bradley Walker Tomlin. Sharing, at least in theory, the surrealist distrust of consciously wrought design, this group has sought to work instinctively, letting the brush (or the dripped paint) wander over the surface until it captured, by the character of its patterns, an expression of conscious, or more often subconscious, states of mind. This one aspect of their work—its automatism—has made it our most controversial and most frequently attacked branch of modern painting, but in practice the technique of these artists has not been quite so uncontrolled as it sounds in theory, and their art is far from formless. Its strength lies in an evocative suggestion of symbols and elusive meanings, and it has produced, in the hands of the different painters, styles of marked individuality.

In spite of its wider acceptance by artists and public, abstract art is still not popular. Periodically it is accused of being "dehumanized," a refuge from reality, a cult of obscurity. Of course abstraction has its limitations. It cannot easily treat concrete themes like the moods of nature or social justice, and it seldom has regional color. But all serious abstract painting does deal with reality, often profoundly, because the very nature and relation of its forms are symbols of the nature and order of life, and it is only through order that life acquires meaning. Nor can the abstract method be accused of anti-humanitarianism simply because it does not portray human beings. The preoccupation of much abstract art with the subconscious is comparable to psychoanalysis, except that it is intuitive rather than analytical. At the opposite extreme, geometrical abstraction is an exercise of pure intellect, though again on an intuitive rather than a scientific plane. Together they are the symbolic expression of man's sensual and rational nature.

Obviously abstract art deals with reality on a much more general level than representational art. It cannot, alone, fulfill the legitimate need for other kinds of painting that are concerned with more specific experience. Already there are some signs of slackening in the abstract tide. Whether that occurs or not, abstraction has enriched American culture not only with a notable body of work but also with perceptions and techniques that will long prove useful. Indeed, many of these have already found their way into our more naturalistic painting where their influence, together with that of surrealism, has done much to free the artist from conventional limitations. The visionary art of Morris Graves and the poetic fantasies of Loren MacIver are examples. Neither painter could be called abstract, neither could be called surrealist; yet it is doubtful whether their free play of forms and of fancy would have been possible without the example of those movements.

Our contemporary expressionists have also been affected, though to a lesser extent, by abstract and surrealist influences. Expressionism, as one of our earliest and most durable modern movements, had of course its own tradition of freedom and radical improvisation. When, late in life, one of its pioneers like Marsden Hartley finally reached the full measure of his powers, he owed little to our current abstract and surrealist

schools. On the other hand, there has been a noticeable trend towards a more abstract style, and occasionally towards more fantastic content, on the part of such diffterent expressionists as Kuniyoshi, Watkins, Weber, Lebrun, Lawrence and Hyman Bloom. In their case it involved no very great change in direction, only a somewhat different emphasis, but they seem to have responded, at least in part, to the prevailing atmosphere of our day. Virtually all of them have done their finest work in this period and thereby maintained expressionism as a major movement in our contemporary art.

Actually it is a little misleading to call expressionism a movement because its members have never been bound together by the same sense of kinship that one finds among the abstract and surrealist painters. Stylistically, they have in common only the fact that they use free distortions for expressive effect—but the degree and nature of their distortions vary immensely. In attitude they are generally romantic, but in subject matter they have no common program whatever (except for the social protest group) and range over the whole of life and death, of war and peace, of nature and religion. Probably few of these men ever think of themselves as expressionists but only as artists who are using both modern and conventional means to paint, with the utmost skill at their command, those things that matter most deeply to them. After half a century of steady development, expressionism has lost much of its revolutionary aspect and has become a widely accepted part of our artistic tradition.

Many other kinds of painting have continued to flourish during the last fifteen years. Except for militant regionalism, which has much abated, virtually all our earlier trends have persisted and, in several instances, have reached a greater power and maturity than they had achieved before. Some of the finest paintings of the American scene are to be found in the late work of Hopper, Marin, Hartley and Burchfield, though numerically the movement has probably dwindled. Social protest painting has changed its sights somewhat, but has still found ample targets in war, corruption and human suffering. All its leading figures—Shahn, Evergood, Levine and Grosz—have grown in artistic stature during these years and have, on the whole, become less polemical, deeper in their understanding of human frailty. As a result, the movement has lost some of its bitterness, but it is still primarily concerned with the social relations of men, and it is still, on occasion, a goad to the conscience of society.

At the conservative extreme, stylistically speaking, is a movement of exact, almost microscopic realism which has grown rapidly in recent years. Its genesis is complex and goes back at least to the early 1930's. One of its ancestors was probably Grant Wood's *American Gothic,* and while Wood himself soon abandoned the meticulous style of that picture, a group of quite different American Scene painters—principally Paul Cadmus and Jared French—pushed it in the direction of an even greater realism. Another ancestor was the precisionist painting of the Immaculates which, in Sheeler's hands, had become more and more realistic during the 1930's. Still another ancestor was surrealism and those American artists, such as Albright, Blume and Pickens, who came varyingly under its influence. A final source may have been sharp-focus photography which helped reveal the unexpected patterns of natural forms seen microscopically or in arbitrary perspective. Since 1940 these diverse currents have tended to join in a school of meticulously realistic painters who have been animated by various aims, ranging from playful fantasy to a serious concern—as

with Andrew Wyeth—for the inherent poetry in places and things. At times the movement has seemed a little mannered and eclectic (particularly in its borrowings from early renaissance art or from our own *trompe l'oeil* realists of the 19th century), but most of its members are still extremely young and its eventual direction is far from settled.

In spite of the recent popularity of abstraction, it is apparent that the last fifteen years has produced, in America, a greater diversity of styles, subjects and attitudes than any comparable period of the past. This trend toward diversity has grown steadily throughout the 20th century, which might justly be called the age of individualism in the arts. Individualism is, in one sense, the fruit of democracy because democracy permits each artist to find his own solutions without the restraint of a state-approved set of esthetic standards. But democracy does not, alone, automatically produce diversity—witness the long dominion of realism in our 19th-century painting. It is only when traditional values break down, when old faiths waver and a desperate uncertainty besieges mankind, that the artist rises instinctively to the challenge and seeks new truths by exploring with new tools the many corridors of the human heart and mind. It is a lonely search, but a heroic one.

GLARNER: *Relational Painting,* 1949–51.

Oil, 65 x 52. Whitney Museum of American Art.

FRITZ GLARNER

by Dorothy C. Miller

FRITZ GLARNER is a classicist in a period fundamentally romantic. He has chosen one of the painter's most difficult tasks, to express the dynamism of an age of movement and rapid change in terms of classic equilibrium as found in the relationship of vertical to horizontal, the interplay of rectilinear planes of contrasting size and color. His work is severely nonobjective but it always has its roots in nature, or, as he would say, life. This "life" is that of the modern city, specifically the city of New York. It is a life perceived and felt, not filtered through subject matter, casual observation or conventional associations.

Glarner's composition is built up in areas of pure color, flat, with no hint of perspective, shadow or texture. These areas are related to each other in a counterpoint of color chords, the whole firmly anchored to the limits of the canvas, which, as Glarner says, "is the one fixed factor to which all parts of the painting are constantly related."

The tension and inner dynamism of the composition is keyed to higher intensity by diagonals which maintain the emphasis on vertical and horizontal and at the same time divide the rectangles by forming two quadrilaterals within them. This makes for movement within a closely integrated architecture where the relation between form and space, foreground and background, is so intimate that, to all intents and purposes, they become equivalents, blending into each other as night blends into day.

Glarner was born in 1899 in Zurich, Switzerland, of a Swiss father and an Italian mother. As a child he lived in Paris, Chartres and various cities of Italy. He studied at the Royal Institute of Fine Arts, Naples, 1914–20, living in Italy until about 1923 when he went to Paris. There he studied at the Colarossi Academy, 1924–26. He first exhibited his work in Naples in 1920, Milan in 1921 and Paris in 1926, and held one-man

GLARNER: *Relational Painting, No. 61,* 1953.

Oil, 60 x 40. Duveen-Graham Gallery.

FRITZ GLARNER   225

shows in Paris, 1928, 1930, and in New York, 1931. In 1936 he came to the U.S.A. to become an American citizen. Four one-man shows were held in New York and two in Paris in the past decade. Avant-garde collectors such as Katherine S. Dreier, A. E. Gallatin and Saidie May bought his paintings, as have the Museum of Modern Art, the Whitney Museum of American Art and the Walker Art Center, Minneapolis.

Glarner: *Words are not the painter's means. They cannot express visual dimensions, but they can establish their relationship in time and stimulate the act of looking. They can also suggest some equivalents of the painter's work, what he has learned and experienced, the environment in which he lives and which imbues his work to a certain degree. . . .*

My concern in painting has been to bring about a purer and closer inter-relation between form and space.
. . .

The slant or oblique which I have introduced in my painting . . . determines the space and liberates the form. This may be seen clearly in the circle, the strongest form symbol of oneness. A multiplicity of similar quadrilaterals, one side of each a segment of the circumference, establishes the structure and becomes one with the space. Differentiation is established by the opposition of color and space areas, and the receding and advancing properties of various colors which give a new kind of depth to the space. Differentiation of textures disturbs the unity of a painting of pure relationships. The same texture should be maintained throughout the work. . . .

It is my conviction that this relational painting is part of a step-by-step development toward the essential integration of all plastic art. (From *A Visual Problem,* a speech made at "The Club," 8th Street, New York, February 25, 1949.)

See: J. J. Sweeney, *Fritz Glarner* exhibition catalogue, Pinacoteca, N. Y., 1949. Fritz Glarner, What Abstract Art Means to Me, *Museum of Modern Art Bulletin,* no. 3, 1951, pp. 10–11.

GLARNER:

Relational Painting, Tondo No. 20, 1951–54.

Oil, 47⅜ diameter. Duveen-Graham Gallery.

I. RICE PEREIRA

by John I. H. Baur

PEREIRA: *White Lines,* 1942.

Oil on parchment, 25⅞ x 21⅞. Museum of Modern Art, gift of Edgar Kaufmann, Jr.

BENEATH the exquisite geometry of Irene Pereira's work there lies a profoundly mystical attitude towards the nature of man and his universe. Long before she became a painter this was apparent. A lonely and introspective child, she had visions of the sun as God, wrote poetry and read omniverously. After her birth at Chelsea, Massachusetts, in 1907, the family moved often, finally settling in Brooklyn in 1922. Four years later she took her first art course at Washington Irving High School and decided to become a painter. In 1927 she enrolled in evening classes at the Art Students League, where she studied until 1930. During the same period she married the commercial artist, Umberto Pereira, from whom she received a divorce in 1938. She finished her formal training with a brief period of study at the Académie Moderne in Paris on a trip abroad in 1931–32.

Pereira's first mature work was done on Cape Cod in the summer of 1932. There she painted anchors, wharfs and other ship's gear in a vigorously expressionist style, occasionally varied by flat, semi-abstract patterns. Throughout the 1930's she experimented at length with methods of obtaining various textures in paint and with techniques for painting on glass and on parchment. Much of this was done under the aegis of the WPA, both as an artist on the Federal Art Project and as a teacher in its Design Laboratory.

In 1937 Pereira began to do those strictly geometrical and rectilinear abstractions from which she has seldom deviated since. Her choice was dictated largely by her fascination with the fourth dimensional world of modern physics and mathematics, for which she has sought plastic equivalents. But her method is purely intuitive and her complex designs spring from an inner rhythm,

PEREIRA: *Spring, Twelve O'Clock*, 1952.
Oil, 30 x 50. Henry F. Lenning.

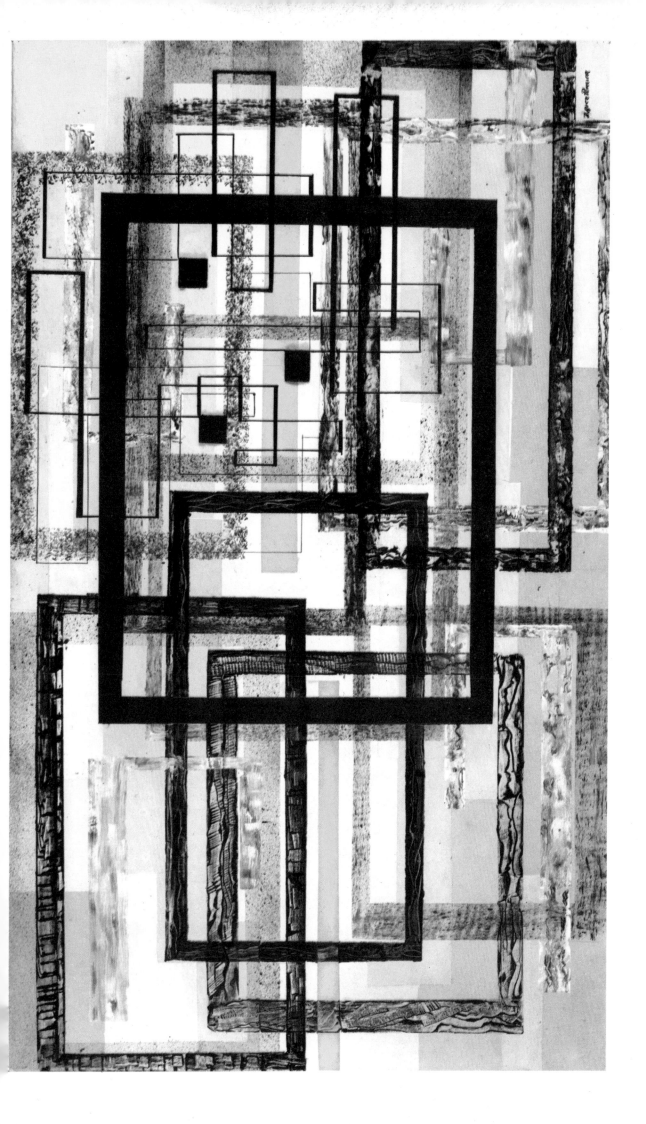

OPPOSITE:

PEREIRA: *Evaporating Night,* 1951.

Oil, 36 x 30. Dallas Museum of Fine Arts.

not from calculation. Holding her rectangles and grids together by the sheer force of her instinctive feeling for dynamic relations, she often seems to suspend them, floating, in a limitless space. Light, which is for Pereira both the male principle and the humanizing element in the vastness of interstellar space, floods through nearly all her pictures, giving them brilliance and emotional warmth. It is especially radiant in the paintings done on several layers of hammered and fluted glass or on parchment stretched over a reflecting background. Only once did it threaten to disappear from her work and that was during the unhappy winter of 1950–51 spent in the gloomy city of Manchester, England, where she had gone to marry her present husband, the poet George Reavey. Since their return to America light has become an increasingly important element in her work, which has also grown more romantic in other ways. Mists of color now escape at times from their bounds and undulate across the backgrounds of certain paintings. In others there is a poetic and a more specific symbolism; *Spring, Twelve O'Clock* is painted in the pale greens of its season, its yellow bands are sunlight, its blurred gray ones are wind. Unlike most geometrical abstractionists, Pereira has made of this highly disciplined style a very personal instrument of romantic expression.

Pereira: *One's work is a mysterious process. Its conscious reality may remain a secret for a long time; maybe forever. The symbol has safely guided my course into the unknown realm of experience. The traveller is just a pilgrim. Sometimes he knows a little more, often less, because values change with each voyage. Sometimes one gets a glimpse of the bridge to eternity before it disappears like a rainbow. Somewhere between exaltation and despair lies the answer. In one sense my work gives structure and dimensions to thought in time. In another sense it is what the eye perceives when it looks inward and feels a firmament set with the jewelled constellations of the time that is man.*

See: I. Rice Pereira, Light and the New Reality, *The Palette,* Spring 1952, pp. 4–13. John I. H. Baur, *Loren MacIver and I. Rice Pereira,* 1953, pp. 37-71.

PEREIRA: *Transfluent Lines,* 1946.

Mixed media on gesso panel and two planes of glass, 24 x 18. Mr. and Mrs. Burton Tremaine.

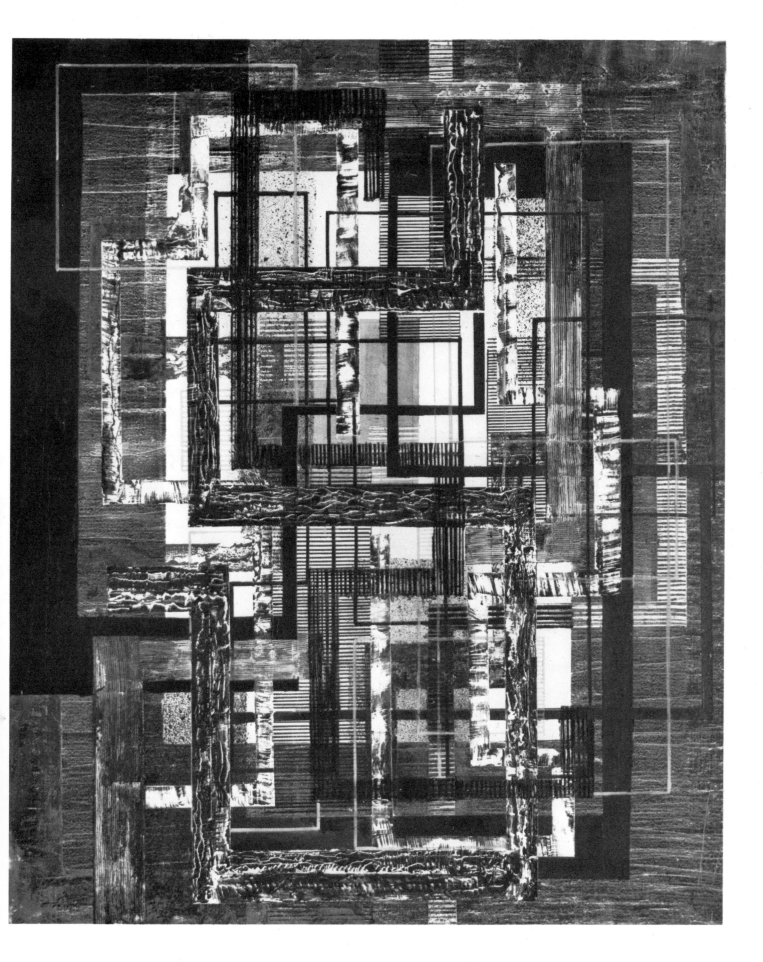

I. RICE PEREIRA   231

WILLEM DE KOONING

by James Thrall Soby

DE KOONING: *Asheville II,* 1949.

Oil, 25⅝ x 31⅞. Phillips Collection, Washington.

IN CONTRAST to his precocious colleagues, Stuart Davis and Peter Blume, Willem de Kooning has progressed slowly toward his vigorous maturity as an artist. Only during the last decade has he developed the rich, turbulent style by which he is now known as a leader among American painters of his generation. Before that he was occasionally heard of as a skilled draftsman in the realist tradition. One learned that he was in no hurry to exhibit his works, that his struggles of conscience were prolonged, that he was determined to understand fully the nature of his creative impetus as an artist.

All this seemed in character with de Kooning's Dutch heritage (he was born in Rotterdam in 1904 and came to this country in 1926). Yet nothing quite prepared us for the authority of his first one-man show, held in New York at the Egan Gallery in 1948. Here was an artist in whom the emotionalism of van Gogh and Mondrian's restraint were combined but left no stylistic trace of either predecessor. Here was a painter whose color was often sombre, whose strong contours were controlled, but whose pictures nevertheless conveyed a sense of tumult and ardor. One found it hard to think of these paintings as abstractions.

After a while they were not. A few years ago the whirlpool forms of *Excavation* began to take on a human configuration, and there evolved the series of pictures collectively entitled *Woman.* The fierce conviction of these images is almost unique in postwar painting here or abroad. They stick like burrs to memory, and already have had a profound effect on younger American artists, eager to move beyond pure abstraction to more specifically human content.

See: Louis Finkelstein, Marin and deKooning, *Magazine of Art,* Oct. 1950, pp. 202–206. Thomas B. Hess, DeKooning Paints a Picture, *Art News,* Mar. 1953, pp. 30–33, ff. James Fitzsimmons, Review of exhibition at the Sidney Janis Gallery and Comment on DeKooning Paints a Picture, *Arts and Architecture,* May 1953, p. 4 ff.

OPPOSITE:

DE KOONING: *Woman I,* 1950–52.

Oil with charcoal, 75⅞ x 58. Museum of Modern Art.

DE KOONING: *Painting*, 1948.

Oil and enamel, 42⅝ x 56⅛. Museum of Modern Art.

234   WILLIAM DE KOONING

DE KOONING: *Excavation*, 1950. Oil, 79 x 100. Art Institute of Chicago.

JACKSON POLLOCK

by James Thrall Soby

IN 1944 Jackson Pollock, born in Cody, Wyoming, in 1912,* held his first one-man exhibition at Art of This Century, the New York gallery of Miss Peggy Guggenheim, his most important early patron. It was apparent to a small group of museum officials, collectors and critics that a hardy and daring new talent had arrived on our art scene. During the past twelve years Pollock has steadily reinforced his position as a central figure in the latest resurgence of abstraction as a dominant force in painting here. The characteristics of early works like *Guardians of the Secret*—intense, nervous energy of line, tumultuous color and slashing, rich surfaces—have been retained. But Pollock has become more and more interested in developing a spontaneous release for his creative personality, eschewing formal values in favor of a quick calligraphy which is convoluted, labyrinthine—and fierce.

Pollock's detractors call his current painting the "drip" or "spatter" school, and it is true that he often spreads large canvases on the floor and at them flings or dribbles raw pigment of varying colors. The fact remains that his technique, if unorthodox and utterly opposed to traditional concepts of the hand-painted oil, suits his idiosyncratic and dedicated purpose. More than that, it is inimitable, as disciples have learned to their sorrow. And Pollock returns at intervals to modeling with the brush, as in *Ocean Greyness*.

The vitality of Pollock's art is its frenzied conviction and its sensitivity to nuances of light and movement, space and balance. Its transcriptions of mood are varied and subtle. His imprint is unmistakable in all his works, but no two of them are really alike. To call these paintings decorations is a misreading of Pollock's intention and achievement. They are, on the contrary, pictures that actively and repeatedly engage the observer, suggesting allusions that trouble more often than they soothe.

*Jackson Pollock died in an automobile accident August 11, 1956.

See: Clement Greenberg, Jackson Pollock, *Partisan Review,* Jan.–Feb. 1952, p. 102. Parker Tyler, Jackson Pollock, *Magazine of Art,* Mar. 1950, pp. 92–93. Robert Goodnough, Pollock Paints a Picture, *Art News,* May 1951, p. 55 ff.

POLLOCK: *Number 3,* 1951.

Oil, 56 x 24. Betty Parsons Gallery.

OPPOSITE:

POLLOCK: *Guardians of the Secret,* 1943.

Oil, 49 x 81. San Francisco Museum of Art.

POLLOCK: *Number 1,* 1948.

Oil, 68 x 104. Museum of Modern Art.

OPPOSITE:

POLLOCK: *Ocean Greyness,* 1953.

Oil, 57¾ x 90⅛. Solomon R. Guggenheim Museum.

POLLOCK: *Blue Poles*, 1952.
Oil, 83 x 192. Dr. and Mrs. Fred Olsen, courtesy Sidney Janis Gallery.

240

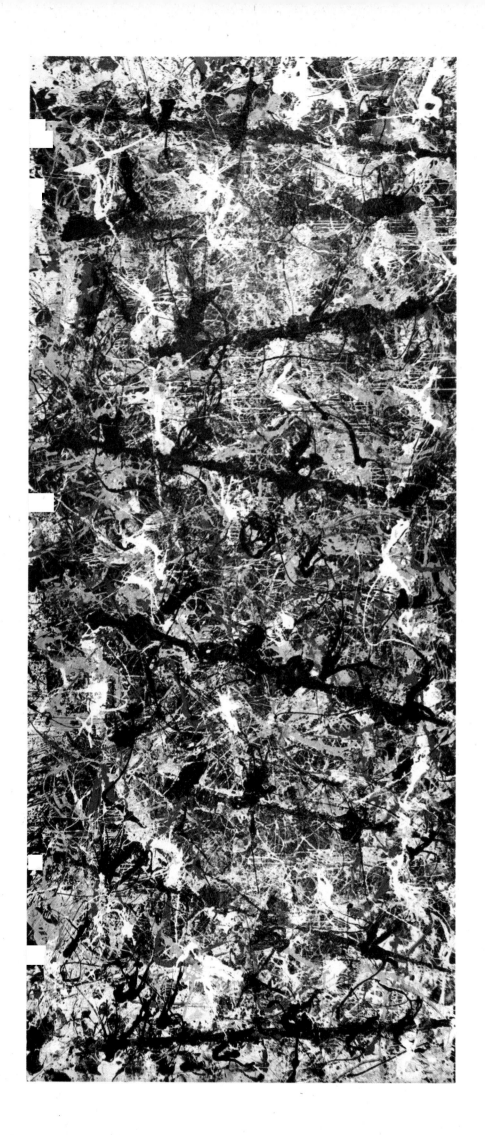

WILLIAM
BAZIOTES

by Dorothy C. Miller

WILLIAM BAZIOTES was born in Pittsburgh in 1912 and grew up in Reading in the Pennsylvania Dutch country. He went to New York in 1933 and studied at the National Academy of Design, 1933–36. Quite as important as formal study in his development have been his contacts with his fellow painters and his own exploration of the work of artists he particularly admires. Among these he has named Piero della Francesca, Titian, Rembrandt, Utamaro, Rubens, Velasquez, Goya, Fragonard, Ingres, Corot, Seurat, Renoir, Bonnard, Matisse and Miro. He says: "The sense of artistic communion is important to my work. . . . There is always unconscious collaboration among artists. The painter who imagines himself a Robinson Crusoe is either a primitive or a fool. The common goal is difficult to

BAZIOTES: *Moon Forms,* 1947.

Oil, 36 x 48. Mrs. Samuel M. Kootz.

BAZIOTES:

The Dwarf,
1947.

Oil, 42 x 36⅛.
Museum of
Modern Art,
A. Conger
Goodyear Fund.

describe, but I do know it is not a certain universal sub-ject matter. However, in the best practitioners of ab-stract painting, I sense the goal when I see the artist has had the courage to live in his time and in his own fashion. And when he has courage, there is *style* in his work. The subject matter in his work can be the tremors of an unstable world or the joy of a summer day. Both are equally valid. Each artist must follow his own star." (From Symposium: The Creative Process, *Art Digest,* January 15, 1954.)

In 1936 Baziotes joined the teaching division of the New York City WPA Federal Art Project. After two years of teaching he transferred to the easel project where he worked during 1938–41. In 1944 in New York he had his first one-man show; he has had a one-man show every year since then, except 1945 and 1949, and was included in *Fifteen Americans* at the Museum of Modern Art in 1952. He is represented in twenty museums throughout the United States and in Tel Aviv, Israel. He teaches at Hunter College, New York.

WILLIAM BAZIOTES   243

BAZIOTES: *Jungle*, 1951.
Oil, 48 x 60. Private collection.

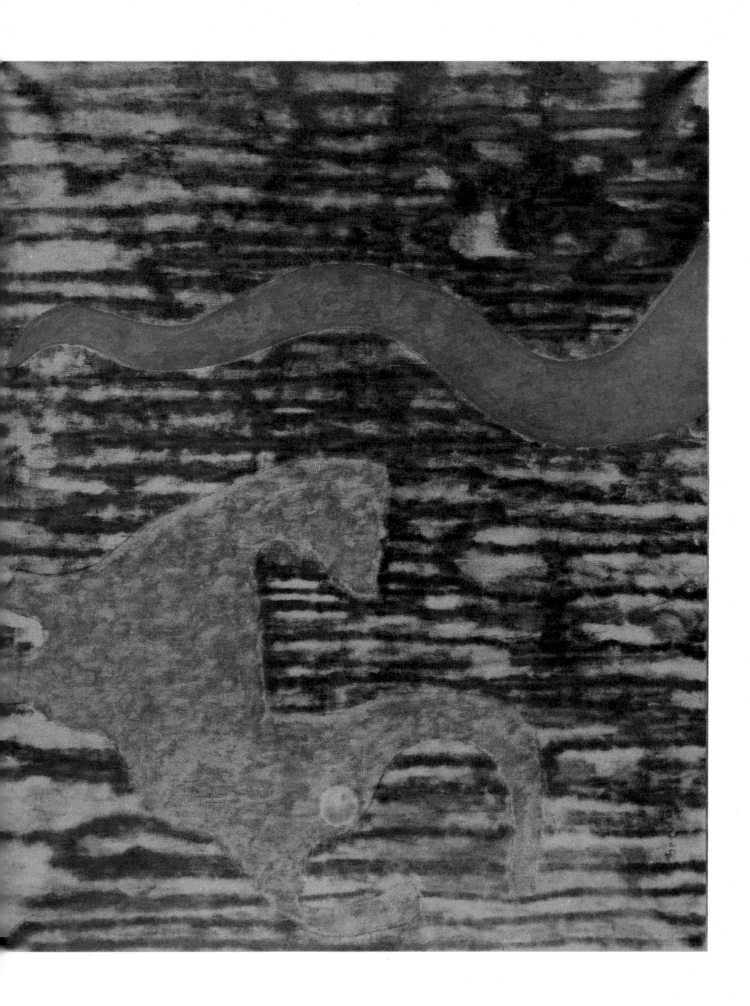

Baziotes: *Painting, for me, is an endless falling in love with life. For me, the visual is everything. To be endlessly surprised. To look at the world with primitive eyes. And then, to go to my canvas with the truth of intuition.*

See: Baziotes, Statement, *Tiger's Eye,* Oct. 1948, p. 55. Baziotes, The Artist and His Mirror, *Right Angle,* June 1949. Museum of Modern Art, *Fifteen Americans* exhibition catalogue ed. by Dorothy C. Miller, 1952, pp. 12–14. Baziotes, Symposium: The Creative Process, *Art Digest,* Jan. 15, 1954, pp. 16, 33–34.

BAZIOTES: *Dragon,* 1950.

Oil, 48 x 40. Metropolitan Museum of Art.

WILLIAM BAZIOTES

ROBERT MOTHERWELL

by Frederick S. Wight

"I DON'T KNOW what I think of that idea. I'd have to paint it and see." Motherwell set out to be a professor of philosophy, strayed into painting. As a result, he is spokesman for abstract expressionism as (in his experience) it developed out of surrealism. His disciplined thinking has afforded active defense for paintings and painters otherwise exposed in their irrationality. It has also doubtless clarified his own work, decanting language and leaving the paint in a pure state.

Motherwell was born in Aberdeen, Washington, in 1915, was able to "draw anything by fifteen, learning from copying High Renaissance masters. . . . Drawing is a matter of internal rhythm. I never had anything to do with a model." He studied philosophy under Ralph Barton Perry at Harvard, aesthetics under David Prall, went to Paris in 1938 for a year of further study, and began to paint. He returned to study at Columbia with Meyer Shapiro, who introduced him to Kurt Seligmann. Through Seligmann he met other surrealists: Ernst, Tanguy, Masson, and most important for him, Matta.

MOTHERWELL:

Pancho Villa, Dead and Alive, 1943.

Gouache, oil and collage, 28 x 35⅞ Museum of Modern Art.

At this time Motherwell was under the influence of Matisse's "bourgeois sensualism," and he had also taken to the use of collage, a technique for the manipulation of forms and textures which has stayed with him. "Now Matta was the decisive influence." He went to Mexico with Matta, began to work in "automatic abstract art," returned after half a year to see the surrealist exhibition at the Whitlaw Reid mansion, when he met Baziotes. He was given a one man show by Peggy Guggenheim in 1944.

Since then he has been seen yearly. Large canvases, mounting symbols which convey an hypnotic life-size effect, establish an art of subconscious imagery under conscious control. Two dimensional as a billboard or a page, its qualities are essentially mural. After a near decade of such personal imagery—in the midst of a communicative life enmeshed in the world about him— Motherwell has had the opportunity to work on a mural scale for a synagogue. This has suited his talent well, offering him a field where the language of symbols (visible thought) is already formulated.

For Motherwell, such painters as Baziotes, Gottlieb, Rothko, Still, Tomlin, are on common ground, which they share with Matta, and Miro—"the greatest artist of the generation after Picasso." He is able to convey the thing which somehow makes them a group, the excited sense that the idiom of an epoch has been captured.

Motherwell: *An artist's "art" is just his consciousness, developed slowly and painstakingly with many mistakes en route. . . .*

Consciousness is not something that the painter's audience can be given; it must be gained, as it is by the painter, from experience. If this seems difficult, then— as Spinoza says at the end of his Ethic—*all noble things are as difficult as they are rare.*

Without . . . consciousness, a painter is only a decorator.

Without . . . consciousness, the audience is only sensual, one of aesthetes. (Robert Motherwell, The Painter and the Audience, *Perspectives USA,* Autumn 1954, p. 112.)

See: D. H. Kahnweiler, *Rise of Cubism,* preface by Robert Motherwell, 1949, pp. vi–viii. Paul Bird, Robert Motherwell, a Profile, *Art Digest,* Oct. 1, 1951, p. 6 ff. Robert Motherwell, Rise and Continuity of Abstract Art, *Arts and Architecture,* Sept. 1951, pp. 20–21 ff.

MOTHERWELL: *The Voyage,* 1948. Oil, 48 x 94. Mrs. John D. Rockefeller, III.

MOTHERWELL: *Fishes, with Red Stripe*, 1954.

Oil, 43 x 41. John M. Cuddihy.

BRADLEY WALKER TOMLIN

by Dorothy C. Miller

TOMLIN:

Number 20, 1949.

Oil, 80¼ x 76. Museum of
Modern Art, gift of
Philip C. Johnson.

BRADLEY WALKER TOMLIN came of English and Huguenot stock. He was born in Syracuse, New York, in 1899. He graduated from Syracuse University in 1921 and won a Hiram Gee fellowship for study abroad. This and a Tiffany Foundation fellowship in 1922 enabled him to spend several years in Europe. He studied in Paris at the Académie Colarossi and La Grande Chaumière, and traveled and worked in France, Italy and England until 1927 when he returned to New York. From 1932 to 1941 he taught at Sarah Lawrence College, Bronxville.

His early work, landscape, figure and still life painting which reflected his studies of the art of the past, of Cézanne and the School of Paris, was exhibited in one-man shows in New York at the Anderson Galleries in 1923, the Montross Gallery, 1924 and 1927, and the Rehn Gallery in 1931. Through the 1930's and in the early 1940's Tomlin worked within the cubist tradition, developing an elegant and soberly decorative style, devoted chiefly to still life, which he exhibited in 1944 at the Rehn Gallery. In this period he painted a mural at Memorial Hospital, Syracuse; in 1946 he won an award at Carnegie Institute's International Exhibition and in 1949 a purchase prize from the University of Illinois.

In the mid-1940's his art began a change of direction. The coolly ordered, rectangular spaces of his canvases broke into freer patterning and a bold encompassing calligraphic line enriched his design. He was soon to experiment with pure calligraphy against a monochrome ground; then, with seeming swiftness, his fully realized, final idiom emerged in a remarkable series of paintings, and Tomlin at once took his place among the leading figures of mid-century American art. He showed these paintings in 1950 at the Betty Parsons Gallery, at the Museum of Modern Art in *Fifteen Americans* in 1952, and again at the Parsons Gallery in 1953.

These late paintings have strong linear relationships and juxtapositions of calligraphic elements over a background space in which the only hint of recession in

TOMLIN: *Number 10, 1952–53.*

Oil, 72 x 102½. Munson-Williams-Proctor Institute, Utica.

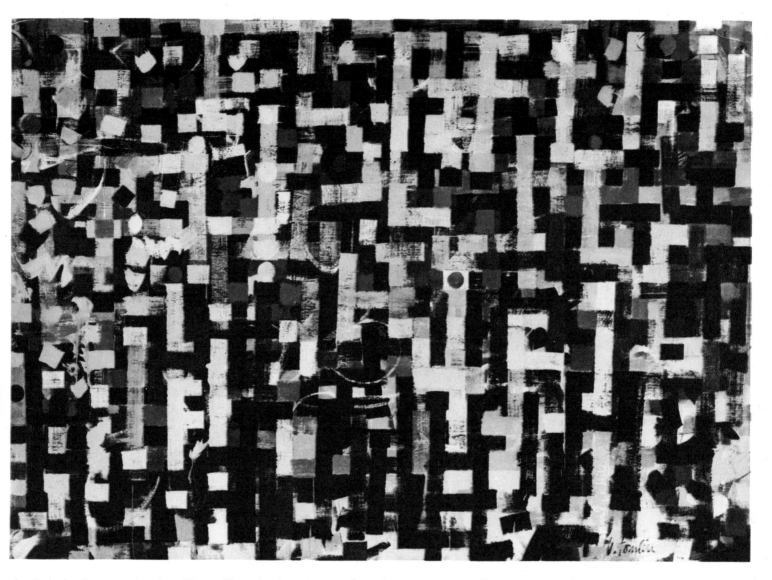

depth is in the use of color. The calligraphy has the suppleness and strength of the Chinese, but the blocky, ribbonlike shapes bear no more than accidental similarity to the Chinese ideogram. The colors are few, the forms restricted, but the mastery of sequence and contrast gives the work a controlled spontaneity, reserved richness and a subtle strength.

Tomlin's death of a heart ailment in 1953 cut short his work at the height of its power. He is represented in a dozen or more major museum and university collections in the United States.

See: Grace Pagano, *Contemporary American Painting,* catalogue of Encyclopedia Britannica Collection, 1946, pp. 120–121. Thomas B. Hess, *Abstract Painting,* 1951, pp. 94, 142, 145, 147. Museum of Modern Art, *15 Americans* exhibition catalogue, 1952, ed. by Dorothy C. Miller, pp. 24–26. Henry McBride, Abstract Report for April, *Art News,* Apr. 1953, pp. 16–17. B. W. Tomlin, Letter to the Editor, *Art News,* May 1953, p. 6.

LOREN MacIVER *by John I. H. Baur*

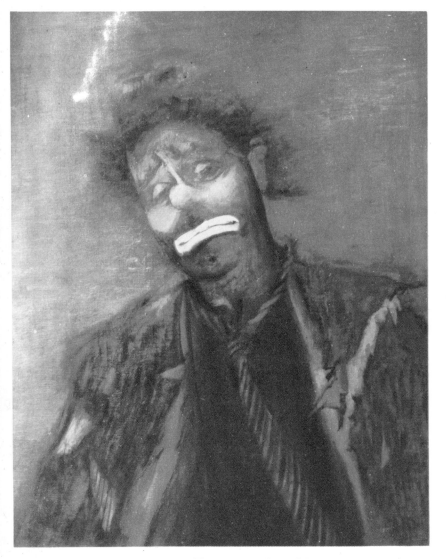

MACIVER: *Emmett Kelly,* 1947.

Oil, 40 x 32. Mr. and Mrs. Roy S. Neuberger.

LOREN MAC IVER is a woman, a notable explorer of New York City and a modern poet in paint. She is also a virtually self-taught artist, her only formal training having been a few lessons at the Art Students League when she was ten. Born in New York in 1909, married at twenty to the poet Lloyd Frankenberg, she has lived in the city ever since, although she and her husband spent ten summers during the 1930's in a driftwood shack which they built on the ocean side of Cape Cod. They have also been to Europe twice, once in 1948, again in 1953–54.

New York has inspired artists in many ways. To the futurists it was a soaring triumph of the machine age; to the social realists it was a grim or picturesque drama of human events. But to MacIver it has been something new and entirely personal—a place where beauty blooms in unexpected corners, where fragments evoke by implication the workings of the human heart. Her subjects have been ashcans, pushcarts, the marks of a child's hopscotch game on blistered pavement, a sidewalk puddle cradling a fallen leaf, the wonderful iridescence of oil stains in the gutter. The human figure seldom enters her work except in rare portraits like that of her clown friend, Emmett Kelly, with its perceptive mood of comedy and pathos. More often people and their emotions are obliquely implied by objects that bear the imprint of human use and suggest intimate associations.

MacIver's mature style has varied greatly, ranging from extreme realism to highly abstract designs. No orderly stylistic evolution is apparent, except perhaps a trend towards more brilliant color, which started after her first trip to Europe when she painted pictures like *Venice* with its rainbow reflections in the blue lagoon. But for the most part her style has varied according to the requirements of each individual subject. Often her pictures require a long second look to decipher fully; the eye is impressed first by her unusual patterns, her shifting color harmonies; only gradually does one per-

MacIver: *Oil Splatters and Leaves*, 1950.

Oil, 25¾ x 56. Mrs. G. Macculloch Miller.

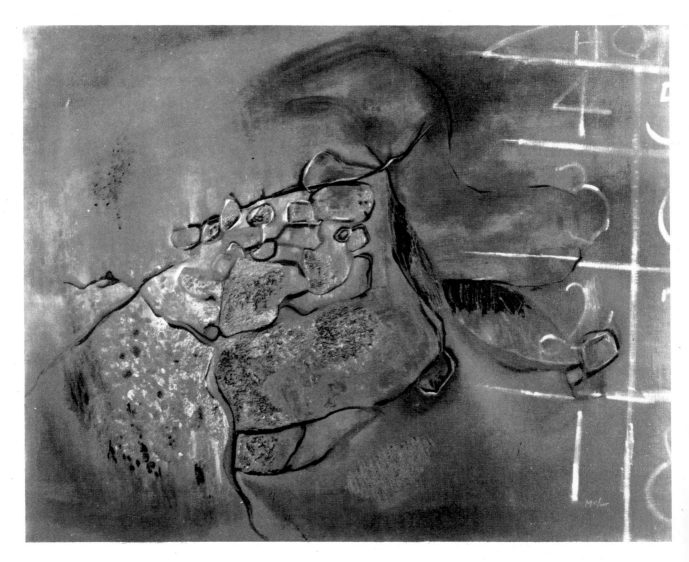

MacIVER: *Hopscotch,* 1940.

Oil, 27 x 35⅞. Museum of Modern Art.

ceive the identity of her forms and read their poetic meaning. MacIver's is a very feminine art of reticence, of intuition and tenderly lyrical feeling.

MacIver: *Quite simple things can lead to discovery. This is what I would like to do with painting: starting with simple things, to lead the eye by various manipulations of colors, objects and tensions toward a transformation and a reward. . . .*

My wish is to make something permanent out of the transitory, by means at once dramatic and colloquial. Certain moments have the gift of revealing the past and foretelling the future. It is these moments that I hope to catch. (From Museum of Modern Art, *Fourteen Americans* exhibition catalogue, ed. by Dorothy C. Miller, 1946, p. 28.)

See: John I. H. Baur, *Loren MacIver and I. Rice Pereira,* 1953, pp. 7–36.

MACIVER: *Les Beaux,* 1952.

Oil, 48 x 40. Art Institute of Chicago, gift of Claire and Albert Arenberg Fund.

MORRIS GRAVES

by Dorothy C. Miller

THE ART OF Morris Graves is an outflowing of religious experience. He has been profoundly moved by the spirituality of the Far East and is steeped in Vedanta and Zen Buddhism. His art has acquired something of the contemplative depth of these religious sources. He has also been deeply affected by the grandeur of the northwest landscape, its wild coast and rocky islands, the great forests and the plants and creatures living there. The art of the Indians, too, and the life of Japan glimpsed in early trips he made as a seaman had much to do with forming his thought.

GRAVES: *Shore Birds,* 1939.

Gouache, 25⅞ x 28⅞. Lee Foley.

GRAVES:

Blind Bird, 1940.

Gouache, 30⅛ x 27.
Museum of Modern Art.

Graves was born in 1910 in Fox Valley, Oregon, an old lake bed high in the mountains where his parents, Seattle people, spent a short time homesteading. The family returned to Seattle and later lived in a town to the north on Puget Sound. At eighteen Graves left school to ship with the American Mail Line out of Seattle, and made three trips to the Orient.

During the depression years he shared a restless, hand-to-mouth existence with other young artists in Seattle, painting, traveling about trying to sell their work, helped by a few interested people. In 1933 he won a prize at the Seattle Art Museum and in 1936 had a one-man show there. At this time he joined the

WPA Federal Art Project, which gave him intermittent support until 1939. His paintings were somber oils of birds, animals, landscape and still life charged with symbolism; but before he left the Project he had been deeply influenced by Mark Tobey, who had lived in the Orient, studied the Chinese brush and developed his calligraphic "white writing." About 1937, Graves turned from oil painting to tempera and wax, ink and gouache on thin papers, finding a means of expression in harmony with his thought. In the four years following, he produced the remarkable series of paintings that brought him immediate recognition in an exhibition at the Museum of Modern Art in 1942.

GRAVES:

Journey, 1943.

Gouache and watercolor,
22¼ x 30⅛.
Whitney Museum of
American Art.

GRAVES:

Wounded Gull, 1943.

Gouache, 25⅜ x 29.
Robert H. Tannahill.

MORRIS GRAVES   263

GRAVES: *Little Known Bird of the Inner Eye*, 1941.
Gouache, 20¾ x 36⅝. Museum of Modern Art.

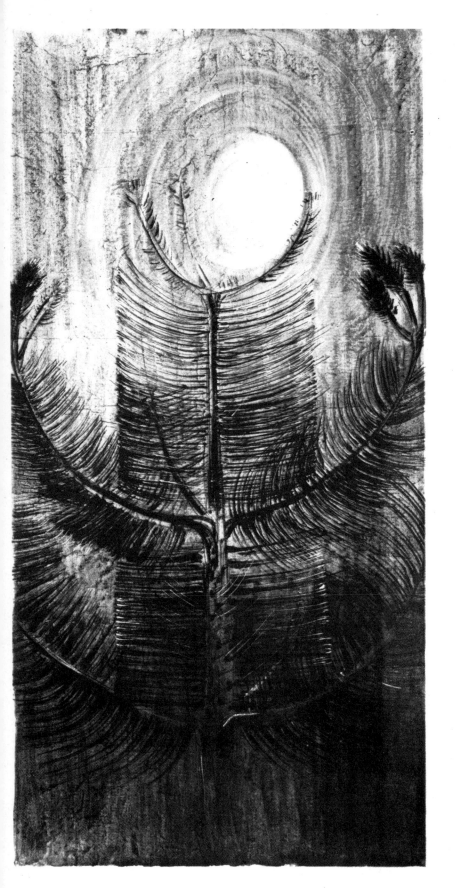

The solitude so necessary to him at this time he sought and found at "The Rock," a high remote spot on Fidalgo Island in Puget Sound. Here he built a shelter in which he lived and worked for years. In 1946 he won a Guggenheim fellowship to work in Japan, but, denied an entrance permit, he stayed in Honolulu painting under the inspiration of the Academy's Oriental collections.

In 1947 he moved away from The Rock and began to design and build a great house in a wood near Edmonds. The next year he went to England on a private commission which fell through; he spent the winter at Chartres painting the cathedral, a series he later destroyed. The Edmonds house, an extraordinary project which seemed to answer the need for a new form, a new discipline, was completed in 1954. Exhausted by its magnitude, Graves went to Japan for several months, then to Ireland where he has worked for the past year and a half.

Graves: *Painting is an experience which is often resisted and is still predominantly a mixture of anxiety and despair. Painting is still the experience of trying to resolve existence—resolve the moment, the day, the year. To the feelings of anxiety and despair is always added a kind of awful delight, a kind of bliss, also a not-caring and a caring simultaneously in an obsessive way, also a sadness and a sense of futility—futility because the experience does not endure, is not final, but must always ebb and be re-experienced . . .*

I wish I could say something clear *about painting, and something about painting better than one knows—it* using you rather than you it. *Also something about the disheartening discrepancy between the vision and the painting—the transferring with paint—the difficult and limited and often impossible medium of paint. That is part of the reason that painting is "resisted"—and too, the ego being so involved when the painting is a failure. To collect one's forces and set them in motion, which so often results in falling far short, is complexly painful, full of desperate and anxious feelings . . . .*
(From a letter, summer, 1955.)

See: Museum of Modern Art, *Americans 1942* exhibition catalogue, ed. by Dorothy C. Miller, 1942, pp. 51–59. W. R. Valentiner, Morris Graves, *Art Quarterly,* Autumn 1944, pp. 250–56. Duncan Phillips, Morris Graves, *Magazine of Art,* Dec. 1947, pp. 305–308. James Thrall Soby, *Contemporary Painters,* 1948, pp. 40–50. Kenneth Rexroth, the Visionary Painting of Morris Graves, *Perspectives USA,* Winter 1955, pp. 58–66. Frederick S. Wight, *Morris Graves,* 1956.

GRAVES: *Joyous Young Pine.* 1944.

Watercolor and gouache, 53⅝ x 27. Museum of Modern Art.

HYMAN BLOOM

by Frederick S. Wight

HYMAN BLOOM is essentially a religious painter, a mystic. His canvases follow through various metamorphoses: sometimes the image is clear, sometimes obscure, sometimes apparently abstract. The themes are great and simple: man's origin—the painter may with some literalness diagram man's first home in the womb, or he may give us his own Jewish origin and spiritual background; and man's death and home in the grave. Appropriately the concern with origins came first. His recent painting of mortality has shocked, as though the canvas were actually a corpse, when it is a *memento mori,* a reminder of the universality of death. He brings us to the edge of a void left by the departure of faith.

Bloom was born in Latvia in 1913, came to this country after the first World War when he was seven, grew up in Boston where he still lives. At a young age he found a teacher in Harold Zimmermann, a backer in Denman Ross of Harvard's Department of Fine Arts, the same two men who were also encouraging the young Jack Levine. Bloom gained from Zimmermann "a technique of working which made it possible to follow the movements of the imagination." At an impressionable age he had a chance to see the work of Rouault, and above all of Soutine, and he set out on a road toward richness and splendor, plangent color, jewel-like effects. It was a rough road through the days of PWA and WPA. "I was used to getting off them and on again." Perforce it was a solitary road. The reading of Spinoza, and above all of Eastern philosophy, condi-

BLOOM: *Archeological Treasure,* 1945.

Oil, 43 x 36. Edgar Kaufmann, Jr.

BLOOM: *The Anatomist,* 1953.

Oil, 70 x 40⅛. Whitney Museum of American Art.

270   HYMAN BLOOM

BLOOM: *Female Corpse, Back View,* 1947.

Oil, 68 x 36. Durlacher Brothers.

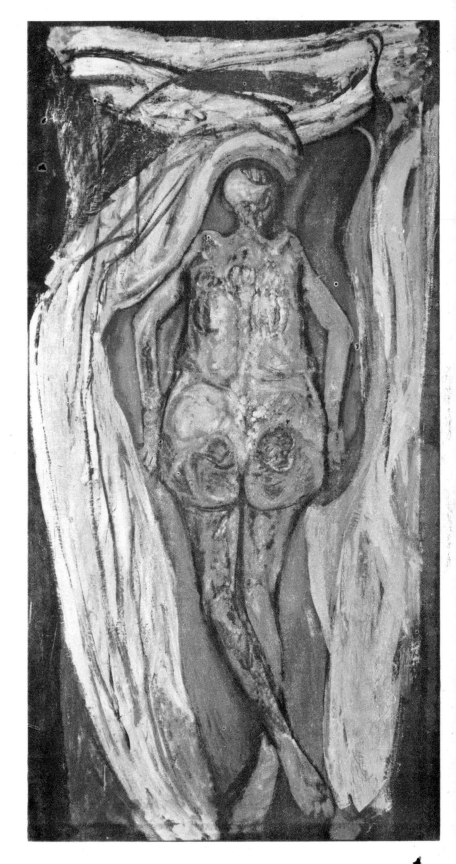

tioned his painting. Image and symbol were essential to Bloom, the architectural irrelevant to his view of life.

Inevitably discussion of Bloom's work shifts to subject matter, which is either hypnotic or horrific; but the subject matter would be intolerable if it were not for the transformation wrought by a great talent. The paintings of mortality have made this talent manifest: everyone has heard because Bloom was saying what none wanted to hear.

Bloom: *For me paint and thought amount to the same thing, or at least they have a goal in common. They are an attempt to cope with one's destiny and become master of it.*

I have been in search of a greater individualization, needing less support from groups.

See: Elaine De Kooning, Hyman Bloom Paints a Picture, *Art News,* Jan. 1950, pp. 30–33 ff. Sydney Freedberg, Hyman Bloom, *Perspectives USA,* Number 6, Winter 1954, pp. 45–54. Institute of Contemporary Art, Boston, *Hyman Bloom* exhibition catalogue, 1954.

OPPOSITE:

BLOOM: *The Synagogue,* 1940.

Oil, 65¼ x 46¾. Museum of Modern Art.

JACOB LAWRENCE

by Frederick S. Wight

JACOB LAWRENCE 273

LAWRENCE: *The Seamstress*, 1946.

Tempera, 21½ x 29½. Southern Illinois University.

JACOB LAWRENCE is still a young painter, and his story is one of self-discovery, of integration with the world about him. He is a Negro. Born in Atlantic City in 1917, he grew up in Harlem where he lived in a settlement house. There was an art workshop and a young instructor. Lawrence began with poster colors, geometrical designs, flat areas. This pattern was right for him. The changes since have been in medium, to gouache, to casein tempera, to egg tempera. He learned through books and reproductions. He never saw an exhibition until he was eighteen.

His life has been a patchwork of difficulties and opportunities. He received a scholarship when he was twenty, had a job on the Federal Arts Project "during the transitional time when I finally knew I would become a painter," applied for a Rosenwald fellowship and received three altogether, from 1940 to 1942. On these grants he did the *Migration Series,* which he feels is his best work.

Lawrence began with an urge to speak of the Negro's situation, has broadened his horizon to take the human situation as his subject. He develops themes: his paintings, being figures of speech, can easily be continued into a series. This means that he is saying in paint what can also be said in words and he must justify the paint, making it the better language. He does this through condensation—"simple, flat, line and mass and no modeling, a pantomime of gesture to create a mood."

When he obtained a Rosenwald fellowship he moved away from his family into a studio. He married, and having done the *Migration Series* and a *Harlem Series,* he too migrated. He went south to the vicinity of Richmond, and then to New Orleans where he painted the *John Brown Series.* Here he had no oppressed feeling. "You don't go into a store or restaurant. You try not to involve yourself. You are on the alert."

During the war he was in the Coast Guard, a steward's mate, then a Public Relations Officer third class.

He was aboard troopships, and he saw the ports of England and France. He was able to paint, and a *Coast Guard Series* resulted. Later he produced a *War Series,* and he has since done a *Hillside Hospital Series*—works of exceptional concentration and power.

Lawrence was at one time interested in theatre scenery, and there is theatre in his art in the best sense. Reality is not *presented* visually but *conveyed* visually by the simplest means, and he achieves our absolute belief.

Lawrence: *Earlier the local situation needed to be painted. Now, I may see something that develops an idea. It means something to me, but how can I express the idea? I try to get a symbol that expresses what I want to say. Figures writing on a blackboard: I want to say something about education.*

A few years ago I was just interested in Negro themes—just that. Now I want to do American history: Washington, Lincoln—there are terrific things to do. A series of scenes from American history within the next five years.

Hope has broadened the scene. The statement is broader, even though it is the same statement.

See: Anon., ". . . And the Migrants Kept Coming." A Negro artist paints the story of the great American minority, *Fortune Magazine,* Nov. 1941, pp. 102–122. Elizabeth McCausland, Jacob Lawrence, *Magazine of Art.* Nov. 1945, pp. 250–54. Aline B. Louchheim, An Artist Reports on the Troubled Mind. *New York Times Magazine,* Oct. 15, 1950. p. 15 ff.

LAWRENCE: *Depression,* 1950.

Casein, 22 x 30. David Solinger.

ANDREW WYETH

by John I. H. Baur

ANDREW WYETH came close to being a child prodigy in art. Born at Chadds Ford, Pennsylvania, in 1917, he was given an early and thorough training by his father, the painter and illustrator N. C. Wyeth. At the age of twelve he did illustrations for the Brandywine Edition of *Robin Hood* and two years later for *The Nub* by Rob White. He was only twenty when he had his first one-man exhibition at the Macbeth Gallery in New York, twenty-seven when he became an Academician. Married to Betsy Merle James, he lives quietly at Chadds Ford in a remodelled schoolhouse, spending his summers at Cushing, Maine.

These two places, where virtually all of Wyeth's life has been cast, are important to his work. Not only have they provided the subjects for his pictures but they have deeply colored his outlook, giving him something of their spare simplicity, an understanding of weather-beaten things, of sun and air and of the underlying tragedy in hard and lonely lives. The microscopically realist style which Wyeth has mastered in his tempera paintings has been a direct response to his love of these places and their people. It is never used to dazzle nor for the sheer joy of imitation. It is a tool for mirroring, as flawlessly as possible, the subtle moods and restrained drama of his chosen themes. His pictures are often symbolic in feeling but the symbolism is essentially pictorial, not literary and seldom explicit. The cruel hooks over *Karl's* head are a vital part of an unusual design; whatever else they may mean is left to

WYETH: *Karl,* 1948.

Tempera, 30⅝ x 23⅝. Mrs. John D. Rockefeller, III.

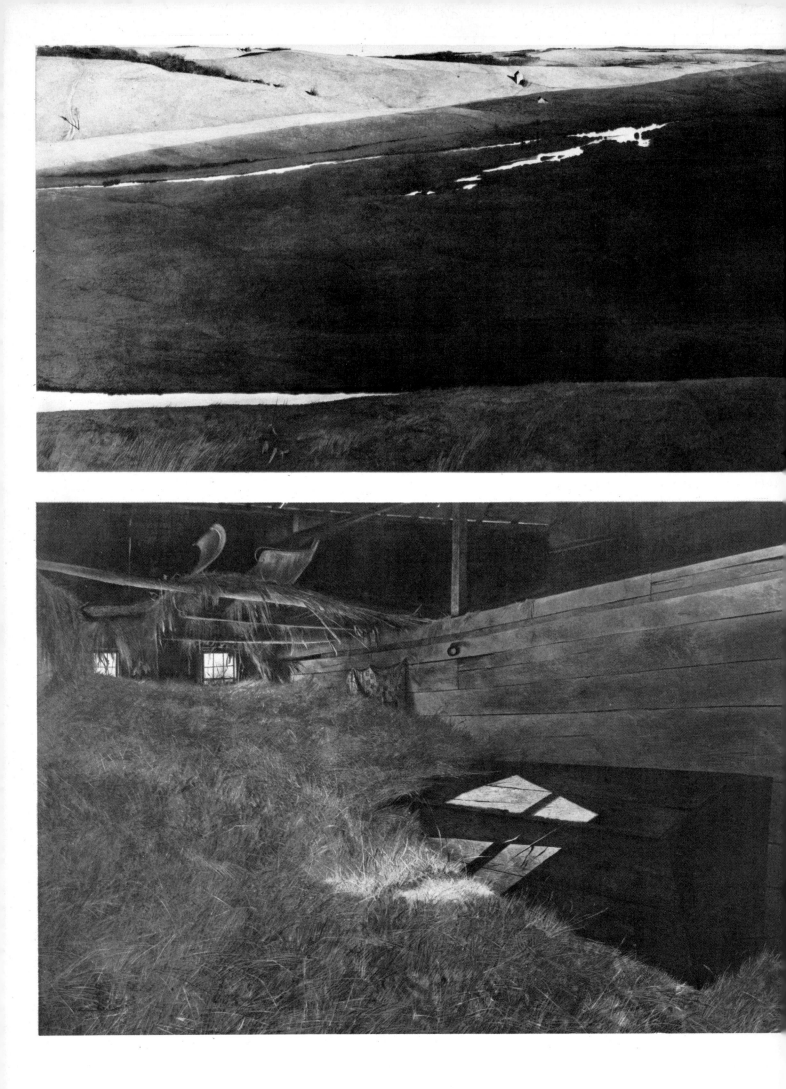

the beholder. The dramatic contrast between the crippled Christina Olson and the sunlit field through which
she crawls has its bleak poetry, susceptible of many
interpretations. Even Wyeth's unpeopled landscapes
are filled with their own distinctive moods, wrought by
an incredibly skillful manipulation of light, perspective,
textures and subdued color harmonies. There is no
doubt that the artist has been strongly influenced by
both the sharp focus and unconventional angles of
modern photography but he has transformed them into
a painter's terms and used them, with the other means
of his craft, to create an emotionally rich record of
American back country.

Wyeth: *Time is valuable to me. It will allow me to
absorb the techniques of the mediums in which I work.
In order to express in truth the basic facts of the world
I behold, I hope to have digested the means of expressing it so thoroughly that the object or subject painted
will become the all important thing.*

See: The Currier Gallery of Art and The William A. Farnsworth
Library and Art Museum, *Andrew Wyeth* exhibition cata-
logue, introd. by Samuel M. Green, 1951. Elaine de Kooning,
Andrew Wyeth Paints a Picture, *Art News,* Mar. 1950, pp.
38–41, 54–6. Parker Tyler, The Drama of Perspective in
Andrew Wyeth, *American Artist,* Jan. 1950, pp. 35–8.

WYETH: *Northern Point,* 1950.

Tempera, 36 x 18¼. Wadsworth Atheneum, Hartford.

WYETH: *Christina's World*, 1948.
Tempera, 32¼ x 47¾. Museum of Modern Art.

280

INDEX OF ARTISTS